KEEPING THE MARCH ALIVE

Keeping the March Alive

How Grassroots Activism Survived Trump's America

Catherine Corrigall-Brown

NEW YORK UNIVERSITY PRESS

New York

NEW YORK UNIVERSITY PRESS
New York
www.nyupress.org

References to Internet websites (URLs) were accurate at the time of writing. Neither the author nor New York University Press is responsible for URLs that may have expired or changed since the manuscript was prepared.

Library of Congress Cataloging-in-Publication Data
Names: Corrigall-Brown, Catherine, author.
Title: Keeping the march alive : how grassroots activism survived Trump's America / Catherine Corrigall-Brown.
Description: New York : New York University Press, 2022. | Includes bibliographical references and index.
Identifiers: LCCN 2022002721 | ISBN 9781479815050 (hardback) | ISBN 9781479815074 (paperback) | ISBN 9781479815081 (ebook) | ISBN 9781479815098 (ebook other)
Subjects: LCSH: Women's March on Washington (2017) | Social movements—United States—History—21st century. | Political participation—United States—History—21st century. | Social action—United States—History—21st century. | Social change—United States—History—21st century. | Political activists—United States—History—21st century.
Classification: LCC HN59.2 .C675 2022 | DDC 303.48/40973—dc23/eng/20220301
LC record available at https://lccn.loc.gov/2022002721

New York University Press books are printed on acid-free paper, and their binding materials are chosen for strength and durability. We strive to use environmentally responsible suppliers and materials to the greatest extent possible in publishing our books.

Manufactured in the United States of America

10 9 8 7 6 5 4 3 2 1

Also available as an ebook

For

my father,

Hans Brown,

a tireless advocate for social justice

CONTENTS

1

Indivisible across Cities

The Many Faces of the Resistance

Donald Trump was inaugurated as the president of the United States on January 20, 2017. The next day, activists assembled in over 400 marches across the United States and around the world to express their unhappiness with the new president and his agenda (Women's March, 2017). These marches were unprecedented in size, bringing together as many as 5.3 million Americans, or about 1.6 percent of the US population (Chenoweth, 2017). The largest marches were in Washington, DC, Los Angeles, and New York City, uniting local activists with fellow marchers from surrounding cities and states. That night, many of these marchers got back on buses to return home to cities and towns across the country. They talked about what would come next, and many were inspired to start local groups. However, the form that these groups took differed greatly across contexts. How groups organized in Atlanta, Portland, and Pittsburgh was very different than how they could (or wanted to) mobilize in Amarillo, Salt Lake City, or Dayton.

Activists getting off buses at home in Salt Lake City were faced with very distinct social, political, and historical contexts for mobilizing than were the activists going home to Portland. In each of these cities, they were met by others who had organized local Women's Marches in the area. In Salt Lake City, about 6,000 participants had gathered for the local inaugural march. Activists filled the rotunda and upper balconies of the state capitol with overflow crowds spilling out onto the lawn. In Portland, Oregon, 100,000 activists had marched from the waterfront through forty-four downtown blocks. The march stretched over two miles and was one of the largest protest events in Portland's history.

Activists from the national event joined those who had mobilized locally to organize groups in each city, with three Indivisible groups founded in Salt Lake City and seven in Portland.

If asked to predict the fate of activism in these cities, most of us would expect that the groups in Portland had a better chance at sustaining the energy and mobilization over time than did those in Salt Lake City. Two years later, however, only two of the seven groups survived in Portland, whereas all three groups in Salt Lake City remained active. This is surprising. Portland has a stronger tradition of activism, had a much larger first Women's March, and had founded more Indivisible groups. However, these groups were less likely to survive until the second anniversary event. Salt Lake City is a much more difficult context in which to organize, had a smaller initial event, and had founded fewer groups. Yet all the Salt Lake City groups survived past two years. What explains these outcomes?

I argue that the different local contexts in the two cities provided distinct opportunities and challenges for activists. Within these different contexts, activists made strategic choices about how to organize and mobilize. They made decisions about (1) tactical selection and diversity, (2) the use of coalitions, (3) practices to facilitate individual engagement, and (4) the use of online technologies. These decisions matter. They affect a group's ability to organize over an extended period of time, whether a group grows and builds alliances, and even whether a group survives.

The comparison of the groups in Salt Lake City and Portland illustrates the significance of each of these four core decisions. Local groups make different choices, and the outcomes are reflected in their fates. First, Salt Lake City and Portland activists deployed very different tactical repertoires. The Salt Lake City Indivisibles engaged in a wide diversity of tactics and were flexible with these tactics over time. Groups in the city focused mostly on electoral campaigns in the first year, lobbying their local congressional representatives. However, it became clear that the local elected officials in these cities were not particularly receptive to this lobbying. In response, the groups shifted to engaging in voter registration in an attempt to elect more sympathetic representatives. The Salt Lake City groups engaged in a wide variety of tactics, such as hosting talks at the local library, social events, and postcard campaigns. The diversity of their tactics, and their willingness to change tactics over time, was a critical component of their success.

The groups in Salt Lake City also engaged extensively in coalitions, with over 85 percent of the events of each of the three groups in the city involving working with partner organizations. Because of the more conservative context in which they were organizing, these groups were careful to create a particular form of broad and nonpolitical coalition. The Salt Lake Indivisibles often cooperated with charities, local libraries, businesses, and other nonpolitical groups and explicitly did not engage in political activities or partnerships. This worked effectively to normalize activism in a community where there were fewer past participants and there was some trepidation about engaging in protest.

The groups in Portland organized within a very different context, but they also made different strategic decisions. In general, the groups in Portland engaged in a narrower and more specialized tactical repertoire. They almost exclusively hosted large protest events and were less flexible with their tactics over time when the context or the interests of their members changed. In addition, the groups in Portland were less likely to work in coalitions with other groups. Only two of the seven groups cooperated with other organizations and did so inconsistently. This created a context where groups worked mostly in isolation and there was not widespread cooperation across the city. And, while the groups were able to host a number of very large events, the groups were much less likely to survive over time.

The groups in Salt Lake City and Portland also managed recruitment very differently. Many of the Salt Lake City activists were new to engagement and came from diverse political backgrounds, including self-defined Independents and even some disenchanted Republicans. Because of the relatively smaller pool of past progressive activists, and the ideological diversity of the organizers, the Salt Lake City groups worked extensively to attract others new to engagement and to frame their group in a way that welcomed the broadest range of people. They did this by focusing on consensus issues, such as gerrymandering or "good governance," and by offering diverse ways for people to engage, from low-cost postcard writing to higher intensity door-to-door canvassing. They also worked to make activism fun and easy: they paired people up with others to register voters or go to town halls, focused on training members to write letters or go door-to-door, and allayed any anxiety that might come with participation. Because the Salt Lake City activists knew that they did not have a deep pool of potential new recruits, they spent considerable time fostering the retention of their members.

In Portland, the organizers were very focused on mobilizing large and vibrant events. In many ways, the wealth of potential activists in Portland initially seemed to be an asset, and it certainly enabled the organizers in the city to host large marches and rallies. However, this perceived endless pool of potential activists also encouraged leaders to spend less time in establishing organizations, coalitions, and online communities that could foster the continued participation of members and the longevity of the groups over time. In addition, the wealth of potential activists in Portland created a situation in which organizers did not feel the pressure to moderate their messages or strategies to attract a broad range of members. Instead, these groups tended to embrace increasingly progressive messages over time, removing members who were seen not to meet their ideological standards. This resulted in high levels of infighting in many of the Portland groups as activists argued about ideology and worried that the group was moderating its views for broader appeal. The highly conflictual atmosphere in many of the groups made the continued engagement of members, and the survival of the groups, less likely.

As the comparison of these two very different cities illustrates, the local context shapes the opportunities and challenges that activists confront as they work to mobilize and bring about social and political change. This book focuses on how political context shapes grassroots activism at the local level. Large national events, such as the Women's March and the other protest events that followed it in Washington, DC, are a critical part of the larger Resistance movement that swept the country between 2017 and 2020. These large events are often the match that sparks a wave of contention. However, in order to understand this widespread and influential wave of mobilization, we must also examine how activism happens across the diversity of cities and towns in the United States. These sites have been the focus of little research, yet they are where the majority of people participate in everyday activism. They are the social movements' lifeblood; only through understanding these local contexts can we truly comprehend the full extent of this mobilization and its impact.

The Resistance

The initial Women's March in 2017 was unprecedented in size and visible in cities and towns across the country, including in Portland and Salt Lake City. This extraordinary level of engagement was inspiring to many on the left, who felt disheartened by the results of the election and passionate about a more progressive agenda. However, many activists began to wonder how this mobilization could be sustained until the midterm elections of 2018 and the next presidential election of 2020. They were right to be concerned. Research, and the experience of many activists, tells us that it is often hard to sustain the momentum of a campaign over time.

Large coordinating organizations around the country, such as Indivisible and Swing Left, were attuned to these challenges and worked diligently to create infrastructures to support continued engagement. Indivisible, for example, began with the online publication of a manifesto called *Indivisible: A Practical Guide for Resisting the Trump Agenda* by Leah Greenberg and Ezra Levin. This guide went viral and inspired citizens across the United States to organize into local Indivisible groups working to counter the larger conservative agenda they felt was sweeping the nation after Trump's electoral win. Over time, Indivisible formalized into a national nonprofit organization aimed at bringing together local volunteer-led groups engaged in progressive advocacy and electoral work at the local, state, and national levels (Indivisible.org, 2020). The national organization works to harness the power of local Indivisible groups and offers advocacy and policy expertise. It also provides an online tool to help potential activists find others in their area who want to engage in progressive mobilization (Brooker, 2018; Greenberg and Levin, 2018).

Organizations like Indivisible were critical in creating and maintaining the Resistance over the next years. The first year of mobilization, 2017, saw at least twelve large-scale national marches, including the Women's March. Some of these protests continued to focus on issues related to gender, such as A Day without a Woman and the Equality March. Many others expanded the agenda by focusing on immigration and racial equality, such as the protests against the Muslim travel ban, in support of Deferred Action for Childhood Arrivals (DACA), and for racial justice. Activists also united in campaigns again corruption and for ethics in government at events such as the Tax March, the March for Truth, and the Impeachment March. The People's Climate March, the March for Science, and local mobilization in support of the Affordable Care Act (ACA) were also critical events in this period of mobilization.

The wave of contention that was labeled the Resistance included individuals and groups who worked to challenge the Trump administration and its policies. The Resistance has been the focus of an expanding body of research that highlights its massive size and diversity (Beyerlein et al., 2018). It is widespread across cities and states (McKane and McCammon, 2018) and is vibrant in suburbs, small towns, and rural areas (Gose and Skocpol, 2019; Putnam, 2019). The Resistance also organizes around multiple issues (Fisher, Jasny, and Dow, 2018; Gose and Skocpol, 2019). In fact, the founders of Indivisible, Greenberg and Levin, explicitly say that they modeled their organization after the earlier multi-issue Tea Party movement on the right (see also Andrews, Caren, and Browne, 2018; Beyerlein et al., 2018; Skocpol and Tervo, 2019). Two books published on this wave of contention, *The Resistance* (Meyer and Tarrow, 2018) and *American Resistance* (Fisher, 2019), offer in-depth examinations of how these newly founded groups interacted with preexisting social movement organizations (SMOs) and created widespread alliances across the political left.

Research on the Resistance has mostly focused on large professional organizations and large-scale protest events, particularly those occurring in cities such as Washington, DC, and New York (except see Gose and Skocpol, 2019; Putnam, 2019). While these organizations and events are clearly critical to the overall wave of contention, they are not the only venue in which individuals are mobilizing. Many local activists are working at the grassroots level in smaller cities and towns across America. Moreover, despite the attention given to these large events, I argue that the everyday activism at kitchen tables, local pubs, and city halls across the country is what animates this larger wave of contention. These activists are critical to movement success and this study focuses on their agency and efforts.

Organizing across Contexts

How do activists make decisions and navigate their local contexts? This is a critically important focus, because these decisions are linked to the success of groups—whether they can mobilize people to the streets, town halls, or other events, and whether they are even able to survive over time. I argue that there are four main sets of decisions that activists must make that account for the mobilization and durability of groups over time: tactical selection and diversity, the use of coalitions, practices to facilitate individual engagement, and decisions about online organizing. In each of the following chapters, I examine how thirty-five Indivisible groups founded in ten US cities navigated their local contexts by making strategic choices in each of these areas.

I begin, in chapter 2, by examining the importance of tactical selection. Activists make strategic choices about what they will do: will they protest on the streets or host town halls, register new voters or organize a phone bank? This chapter asks three main questions. First, how do groups select the *type* of tactic in which they will engage? In particular, I focus on the use of protest and electoral tactics in comparison with other, less political tactics. Second, what is the effect of engaging in a *diversity* of tactics or specializing in a smaller set of tactics? Finally, what are the implications of having *flexible* or consistent tactics? I consider how and why groups make these tactical choices and the implications of these choices for group outcomes, in particular the number of events they host and their propensity to survive over time.

I find that engaging in more protest and electoral tactics is associated with having more events and surviving over time. However, what is even more important than the specific tactic selected is the diversity and flexibility that groups have in their tactical repertoires. Engaging in a diversity of tactics is very important because it helps groups attract new members. It also helps them retain members because they are less likely to burn out. Tactical consistency is also very useful when paired with engaging in protest and electoral tactics. This was particularly true in larger and more liberal cities. In smaller and more conservative areas, groups benefited from being more flexible in their tactics. The differing ways that groups used tactics, and their consequences, highlight the importance of local context for the Indivisible groups in this study.

Chapter 3 focuses on the use of coalitions among the Indivisible groups in the study. Creating a coalition is a powerful tactic for a SMO, and the development of coalitions has long been understood as a critical way that groups and causes can mount successful campaigns and survive over time (McAdam, 1983; Meyer, 2004; Staggenborg, 1986). The first Women's March was based on a coalition of groups working together for a set of progressive causes. Some of the groups that formed after these marches continued to engage extensively in coalitions, working often with other groups in their areas, while others worked mostly alone.

I find that engaging in coalitions with other groups was a very effective tactic, and groups that worked in coalitions more often tended to mobilize more events and were more likely to survive over time. However, I find that the form that coalitions take differs greatly across contexts. In areas with long and active histories of engagement, groups are more likely to join coalitions, and these coalitions often take the form of what I label a "supercoalition." Supercoalitions work to accumulate resources and channel them to existing groups, sometimes even those outside of the coalition itself. In contexts with less history of activism, groups tend to engage less often in coalitions. However, when they do employ this strategy, they foster a distinct form of broad and nonpolitical coalition, often explicitly partnering with civil society groups and eschewing partisan activities. This chapter highlights the effectiveness of coalition strategies while also arguing that the ways in which this tactic is used differs greatly by city context.

Attracting new activists and maintaining the engagement of members over time are always struggles for SMOs. Chapter 4 focuses on the strategies that groups use to attract and retain members, and assesses the consequence of these decisions for group survival. SMOs are engaged in the dual functions of mobilizing and organizing (Han, 2014). Mobilizing is the transactional focus on maximizing the number of people engaged in civic action whereas organizing is the transformational focus on developing the capacities of people to engage with others in activism and become leaders. Organizations can select to focus on one of these tasks over the other and this decision can have important implications for both the group and its members. In this chapter, I examine how groups across the ten cities worked to attract and retain their members, focusing on mobilizing and/or organizing.

I found that groups in liberal cities and cities with larger populations tend to focus on mobilizing, sometimes at the expense of organizing. Groups in these cities often spend most of their energy mobilizing large events and tend to have a more progressive message, as they had less need to work to appeal to people across the political spectrum. However, these groups did not tend to expand activist circles and had higher rates of turnover because there was less focus on retention and easing the burdens of activism. In smaller or more conservative areas, activists often struggled initially as there were fewer potential recruits to mobilize and more local resistance. However, when leaders in these less conducive contexts were strategic, they could create strong and vibrant organizations through seeking new members outside traditional progressive circles. They also tended to focus more on retention, making engagement fun and sustainable for people with work and family responsibilities. As a result, some groups in the smaller and more conservative areas were able to very effectively mount campaigns because they were focused initially on organizing and turned only later to mobilizing.

Chapter 5 examines the use of online technology, particularly social media, among the Indivisible groups at the core of this study. One of the most significant changes in modern mobilization has been the rise of online activism, and this new mode of organizing profoundly shaped the wave of resistance that is the focus of this book. The initial Women's March was organized online as groups around the country rented buses to take activists to Washington, DC, or mobilized people in their local communities. All the groups in this study engaged in mobilizing through Facebook. However, the extent to which the Indivisible groups were able to harness the capabilities of social media was a product of both the interests and skills of the groups' organizers. Chapter 5 explores online mobilization and asks three main questions. First, is the amount of engagement online related to a group's ability to mobilize activists offline? Second, how does the relationship between online and offline mobilization differ across types of groups and events? And, finally, how does the form of the Facebook page and how it is moderated shape group outcomes? Activists have the choice of whether or not to organize on Facebook or other social media platforms and how to set up their pages and content. I argue that these decisions have important implications for a group's ability to mobilize people both online and offline.

The analysis of the Facebook pages and their events shows that there is a strong and positive relationship between the amount of posting on a group's Facebook page and the number of people who self-report that they are going to an event. Posting online is a particularly strong predictor of engagement in protest events and events that require copresence, where participants must engage together face-to-face. When events are not protests or do not require copresence, having more online engagement in the form of posts is not associated with more people saying they will go to the event. While individual events benefit from having more active engagement online on Facebook pages, there is no significant relationship between the number of posts on a group's Facebook page as a whole and the number of events the group hosts or if the group survives until the end of year 2. I also examine the decisions of activists about how to organize their social media, including the number of organizers and the "open" or "closed" nature of their pages. I find that these decisions have important implications for the engagement of members both online and offline, highlighting the importance of activist decisions for the mobilization and success of their groups over time.

Facebook Pages and Indivisible Groups as a Lens on the Resistance

This book examines the mobilization that occurred after the first Women's March in ten US cities. I bring together qualitative and quantitative data collected from Facebook pages and interviews with activists to understand how groups formed, organized, and survived across these very different city contexts. These groups and activists worked in cities which varied in population size and region of the country (see table 1.1 for the list of cities).[1]

I examined all the Indivisible groups that were founded across ten cities right after the first Women's March. The national Indivisible organization provides tools and resources for local groups, such as policy and political guidance, training guides, and hands-on support for activists. These include, most importantly, the *Indivisible Guide*, which circulated on the Internet after the first Women's March as a roadmap for organizing and setting up a group. Indivisible also has a "Find Your Local

TABLE 1.1. Cities by Population Size and Region

	Population Size	
Geographical Region	Medium	Large
East Coast	Bridgeport, Connecticut	Pittsburgh, Pennsylvania Newark, New Jersey
West Coast	Pasadena, California Salt Lake City, Utah	Portland, Oregon
Midwest	Dayton, Ohio Springfield, Illinois	
South	Amarillo, Texas	Atlanta, Georgia

Group" tool that helps people find places to engage by providing lists of local groups through a zip-code search. The "Find Your Local Group" tool has been instrumental for connecting activists, and potential activists, to one another and the movement. Because these groups are all tied together, at least loosely, by a similar ideology, they offer a unique opportunity to compare how the ways that groups mobilize are shaped by the local context. The way that groups enacted the vision of Indivisible differed greatly across cities, and this research is focused on explaining these differences.

One month after the first Women's March, on February 20, 2017, I searched for Indivisible groups in the ten cities through the "Find Your Local Group" tool.[2] The search yielded thirty-five groups with Facebook pages in these cities. While most of the Indivisible groups in this analysis were founded at or right after the first Women's March, some of the groups were preexisting organizations that signed up to be Indivisible groups in early 2017. These Facebook pages provided the primary data for my initial analysis. I chose these data for four reasons. First, only one Indivisible group in the ten cities I selected did not have a Facebook page. Second, it was the most popular social media platform among these groups; those without a Facebook page had no social media pages at all. (Two of the groups also had a Twitter feed.) Third, Facebook has global reach and is more popular than Twitter for the general US population (Vasi and Suh, 2016). Finally, Facebook provides a wider range of

TABLE 1.2. Mobilization by City Context

City	Events per 1,000 Population	Mean Attendance	Number of Groups Founded	Group Survival after 2 Years
Dayton	0.17	94	3	33%
Amarillo	0.32	63	2	100%
Springfield	0.36	27	3	100%
Newark	0.41	10	2	50%
Pittsburgh	0.71	143	5	60%
Portland	0.89	179	6	29%
Atlanta	1.22	148	6	100%
Salt Lake City	3.21	160	3	100%
Bridgeport	4.35	140	2	100%
Pasadena	5.46	680	3	66%

capabilities than Twitter, particularly interactive features that are critical for organizing (Mercea, 2013). I collected data from the thirty-five Facebook pages with the use of a Facebook application from February 20, 2017, through February 20, 2019.[3] These data allow me to compare the amount and persistence of engagement across the cities and groups.[4]

In order to gain more information about the activities of the groups, I hand-coded information on all groups and events listed on each of the Facebook pages from January 2017 to January 2019. This yielded data on over 7,000 events. These data allow me to systematically compare tactics and strategies across the groups. I used these data to predict which groups survived until the end of year 1 (January 2018) and year 2 (January 2019).[5] In January 2019, twenty-five (72 percent) of the groups were still active (see table 1.2).[6]

The Facebook data provide a broad understanding of the activities and events of the groups and enable me to compare their mobilization over time. I also conducted interviews with twenty-five leaders and activists in the Indivisible groups to further understand how activists made decisions, the actual experience of participating in the different groups, and the ways that the groups changed over time. The interviews also helped me to better understand how local context shaped, or did not shape, activists' strategic decisions. More information about the interviews, and all the methods used in this study, can be found in the Methodological Appendix. These diverse data shed light on the factors that predict the level of mobilization in the Indivisible groups and their survival over time. They helped me to assess how groups are navigating their local landscapes and how their choices enable them to be successful.

Becoming Indivisible: The Variety of Indivisible Groups across America

It is clear that the progressive activism at the heart of this study was sparked, or at least invigorated, by the 2017 Women's March. Women activists and feminist causes have long been central to a variety of social movements, including labor rights, civil rights, antiwar activism, prison reform, and community safety. Past research also highlights how women's activism and organizing often take the form of street protest, such as the Women's March. This is, in part, because of the traditional marginalization of women from institutional politics and formal political spaces (Codur and King, 2015; Ferree and Tripp, 2006; Molyneaux, 1998; Principe, 2016). In this way, the rise of such a large, coalitional display at the Women's March can be historically understood in relation to these earlier campaigns and tactics.

While women have traditionally supported a variety of progressive causes, what is interesting and unique about this mobilization was that a variety of other groups came to support an event that was so clearly framed as a "Women's March." As a result, there were many men and other groups present at the event within the vast sea of women in their "pussy hats." In addition, the mobilization that followed over the next years continued to be diverse. Berry and Chenoweth (2018) argue that there are four main reasons why such a variety of groups and constituents were able to coalesce under the umbrella structure of the Women's March. First, the early recruitment of veteran organizers and activists into leadership positions for the march enabled the recruitment of other experienced activists and organizers. Second, the highly active social media context of the 2016 presidential election allowed for informal and nonhierarchical recruitment of a large number of first-time activists. Third, the intersectional and intergenerational base of both the leadership and activist groups meant that the frames and tactics used by the march groups across the country were very diverse. And, finally, the singular focal point of resisting Trump provided enough cohesion, even if only temporarily, to mobilize diverse constituencies.

The broad and coalitional strategy used in national and local organizing for the Women's March clearly influenced the rise of other groups that would follow, including Indivisible. Although many of the Indivisible groups were focused on women's issues and feminism, this varied considerably across groups and contexts. In fact, only thirteen of the thirty-five groups (see figure 1.1) were centrally concerned with issues related to gender and feminism in the two years of this study. This figure highlights how these foci were often the sparks that mobilized these groups but were not always the central issues on which they worked over time. And while many of the groups (about half) did list the second-anniversary Women's March on their webpage, only two of the groups actively engaged with the larger national Women's March organization over time. It is important to understand and consider the feminist and gender roots of this wave of mobilization, and many of the Indivisible groups at the core of this study, while also appreciating the diversity of the causes at both the initial march and in the years to follow within this larger wave of resistance.

The Indivisible groups at the heart of this study varied greatly. While all of the groups were active immediately after the first Women's March in 2017, their histories and trajectories diverged dramatically. Almost a third of the groups were preexisting organizations that were active before the first Women's March. Before 2017, these ten groups focused on women's issues as well as labor rights and racial justice. After engaging in the first Women's March, they listed themselves through the Indivisible

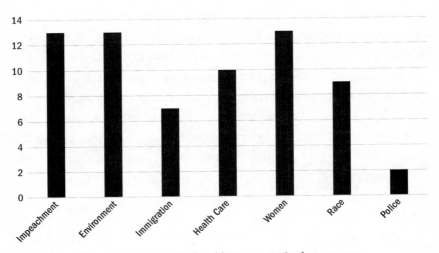

FIGURE 1.1. Main Issue Areas for Indivisible Groups in Study, 2017–2019

"Find Your Local Group" tool to attract new members and engage in the larger Resistance movement. The majority of the Indivisible groups at the core of this study were founded after the first Women's March. These twenty-five groups were spurred to action by the events of January 2017 and were founded to keep the energy and enthusiasm of the march alive within their local communities.

While the Women's March was, obviously, centrally concerned with feminist and women's issues, the Indivisible groups that came next focused on a wide variety of issues on the political left. Figure 1.1 shows the central issue foci of the groups in the 2017 to 2019 period of this study. Many groups had multiple issue areas upon which they focused, such that there was a total of seventy-six areas of focus across the thirty-five groups. Given these groups' connection to the Women's March, it is not surprising that the most common focus was women's issues. However, both impeachment and the environment were also the focus of thirteen groups, equal to the attention on women's issues. Health care was a core issue for ten groups, race was central to nine groups, and immigration was a primary focus of seven groups. Finally, two groups focused on issues surrounding police abuse and corruption.

The Indivisible groups in this project were generally quite active in the period from 2017 to 2019. They hosted an average of 107 events over the first year. This is a remarkably high level of mobilization—about one event every three days. However, the average is deceptive. There was wide variation in how active the groups were, with five groups hosting fewer than ten events in this two-year period and twelve groups hosting 100 or more events in the same time frame. This variation is one of the core foci of this book—what explains why some groups were much more active than others in this period?

The groups also engaged in a wide range of tactics, from protests to town halls, organizational meetings to social events. On average, about a quarter of all group events were protests. Electoral tactics, such as town halls and voter registration, accounted for only 7 percent of group tactics on average. However, there was also wide variation in group tactical repertoires, as illustrated in figure 1.2. And, counter to what most research

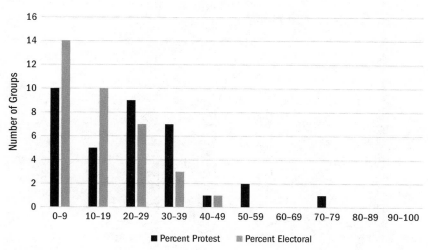

FIGURE 1.2. Protest and Electoral Activity as Percentage of Tactics, by Group

has suggested, most groups engaged in a variety of tactics, including both electoral and protest activity.

It is important to note that cities and towns with longer and more active histories of social movement activism tended to have more Indivisible groups founded.[7] There were twenty-three Indivisible groups founded in these five cities, and only twelve founded in the five cities and towns with less history of engagement. However, it is notable that the survival rate was almost the same across these two types of contexts—two-thirds of groups survived over time, unrelated to the history of activism in the area where they mobilized. This is, in part, because of the agency of activists to make decisions about how and when to mobilize. Even when working in difficult contexts, with less history of engagement, activists can make strategic choices that enable them to successfully mobilize and survive. And these decisions are the focus of this work.

The Women's March in 2017 inspired a large and diverse wave of activism. Much of the interest from media and public observers has focused on massive events in a few large cities, such as Washington, DC, and New York. These events are clearly critical parts of the Resistance. However, they do not tell the whole story of this wave of contention. I argue that the way that this mobilization manifests itself differs widely across local contexts. Examining these local contexts and the grassroots groups that work within them is critical to understanding this larger wave of contention and its impact. This focus on the grassroots is essential. Most people only see and experience activism at the local level, and this shapes their perceptions of the political environment in the country as a whole. The role of the local context in this recent wave of mobilization is not well understood and this book focuses on this important issue. Throughout the next four chapters, I examine how activists navigate these local contexts and make critical decisions related to tactical choices, the use of coalitions, practices for facilitating individual participation, and using online technology. By comparing how activists make these choices across contexts, we can better understand how and when activists are able to mount and sustain mobilizations in their communities.

2

Deciding Whether to Diversify

Tactical Choices and Group Survival

After the first Women's March, activists across America were faced with a difficult decision—what to do next. They could continue to hold protest events or move to other tactics like town halls, letter writing, or online mobilization. Groups faced this decision with different resources at their disposal and in contexts that were more or less conducive to progressive activism. And the decisions that they made had important implications for their ability to mobilize their members and survive over time.

The activists in Amarillo, Texas, were mostly new to engagement when they attended the first Women's March in 2017. Maria, one of the founders of Amarillo 1, remembers how she felt after the election of Donald Trump. "I call it the November Nightmare. I stayed in my bathrobe for three days and was just terribly depressed. But then I decided that I could continue to stay on my sofa in my bathrobe or I could get out and get busy and try to fix it." She called a friend and they began to organize the first Women's March in Amarillo. Maria and her co-organizers expected about fifteen to twenty people to join them as they marched to the Potter County Courthouse. In fact, 400 people came out to protest the new president and his policies. The organizers were elated.

Maria and her fellow protesters worked to harness the energy from this event and channel it into establishing an Indivisible chapter in Amarillo. For the first year, Amarillo 1 held meetings every week in a local coffee shop. The group also hosted many protest events, with about 40 percent of its events in that year alone involving protest on the streets of Amarillo. The protests included events in support of local Indigenous rights, women's rights, and the March for Science. However, by the second year, members were becoming burned out with the same events and felt dissatisfied with what they perceived to be a lack of efficacy. As Barbara explains, "It was getting kind of old. Amarillo . . . is definitely a very conservative, redneck area. And the protest, just going out and standing on the street corners and waving signs, that wasn't doing any good."

The group was, in some ways, constrained by the conservative context in which it was mobilizing. The protest events, in particular, drew counterprotests and aggressive responses from bystanders. Melissa explains that "you have people who drive by and say disparaging things and make derogatory remarks, and try to intimidate you. And you get the Stars and Bars crowd, the people who show up with the Confederate flags. So it is very much about intimidation." Barbara agrees that the presence of the "Confederate flag wavers" created problems for the group, but she refused to be deterred. "We just have to work around them. Figure out ways to get things done with minimal interference from them." This did not mean giving up. It simply meant being more strategic in their tactical choices, given the local context.

Amarillo 1 responded by adapting their tactics. The group reduced the number of meetings, meeting only on the first and third Wednesday of the month. And the group came to embrace a wider range of tactics. It still held large marches, such as the second Women's March and an immigration reform protest, Lights 4 Liberty. However, it also started voter registration drives. Group members went to local high schools and universities to register new voters. This strategy was particularly appealing in the conservative local context. Registering people to vote appears nonpartisan. However, by focusing on registering young people and those in less wealthy areas, the group knew that it was likely to be disproportionately registering potential Democratic voters.

The group also became active in electoral politics. As Maria explains, "I think we've evolved. We got away from just being out protesting on the street corners to a real involvement politically in the areas that we feel we could do the most good." This was partly because the upcoming midterm elections in 2018 made electoral tactics more appealing.

However, it was also the result of the rise of Beto O'Rourke on the state and national political scene. O'Rourke called the local leaders of Amarillo 1 in the summer of 2018 about his upcoming visit to the area. They were surprised and delighted to be contacted. Political leaders rarely came through Amarillo as it was considered too conservative to swing an election. This made O'Rourke's seven visits to the city remarkable. The group organized events for all of his visits and was energized by O'Rourke's campaign.

Amarillo 1 also engaged in a variety of issues at the local level. The group lobbied local officials to change the name of Robert E. Lee Elementary, located in an African American area of town. It petitioned city hall to move a statue of a Confederate soldier from its prominent placement in a local park to a museum. The group also incorporated online mobilization into its repertoire of action. It hosted Facebook live events on health care, immigration, and human rights. These actions were particularly useful for members who either had trouble getting to events or who had anxiety engaging because of fear of potential resistance.

Amarillo 1 hosted fifty-six events in the first two years that involved a wide variety of tactics, including protest and electoral activities. It also was quite adaptive over time, changing tactics when necessary. This vibrant group illustrates a number of important lessons about tactical choices. First, a group's tactical choices are shaped by its local context. Amarillo is a very conservative area and activists had to consider the efficacy of their actions, particularly protest, in relation to the resistance they encountered. This context required them to be nimble in selecting a range of tactics that were sometimes contentious, such as protesting on the street, and sometimes apparently non-contentious, such as voter registration. Second, political events can shift which tactics are most useful and appealing to a group. The timing of the 2018 midterm elections and the political opportunity created by Beto O'Rourke's candidacy made electoral tactics more appealing to local leaders and members. Third, engaging in a variety of tactics, and being open to assessing and adjusting those tactics over time, can be critical to group survival and success. There is no best tactic for social movement groups. Group leaders must consider their local context, changing political opportunities, and the identity and structure of their group when selecting how to engage. This chapter examines how groups make these decisions and the important consequences of these choices for group mobilization and survival over time.

Tactical Choices

Activists make strategic choices about what they will do: will they protest on the streets or host town halls, register new voters, or organize a phone bank? These choices are shaped by a variety of factors. Some of these factors are internal to the group, such as the group's resources, identity, or expertise. Other factors are external to the organization, such as the local context or the political opportunities and threats in their environment (McCammon and Campbell, 2002; Meyer, 2004; Van Dyke, 2003). Each of these sets of factors can shape which tactics a group selects, or is able, to use. This chapter focuses on how groups select their tactics and the effects of these decisions for group mobilization and survival over time. I focus on three main components of these decisions. First, how do groups select the *type* of tactic in which they will engage and what is the effect of this decision on group outcomes? In particular, I focus on the use of protest and electoral tactics in comparison with other less political actions. Second, what is the effect of engaging in a *diversity* of tactics or specializing in a smaller set of tactics and how does this affect groups over time? And, finally, what is the effect of having *flexible* or consistent tactics on group outcomes?

In general, I find that engaging in more protest and more electoral tactics is beneficial for groups and is associated with hosting more events and surviving over time. In addition, engaging in a diversity of tactics is an effective strategy for groups because it helps them mobilize members and endure. Engaging in consistent tactics has a more mixed effect. The Qualitative Comparative Analysis (QCA) shows that there are different routes to mobilization and survival. (The QCA analysis is discussed in more detail both later in this chapter and in the Methodological Appendix). One pathway to survival occurs when groups are consistent and engage in political tactics, particularly protest and electoral activities. This route is particularly common in larger cities and in more liberal areas. Groups that changed tactics over time and engaged in a wide variety of tactics can also be successful. This route is much more likely in smaller and more conservative settings. These key routes to mobilizing success are illustrated through examples of Indivisible groups who engaged in these differing tactics. By examining how groups make these choices and the effects that they have, this research illuminates the complex and situational ways that tactical choices matter for social movement organizations (SMOs).

Tactics are the "forms of collective action taken by movement actors" (Meyer and Staggenborg, 2008, p. 213; Ganz, 2004). A group's tactical choices inform their organization's strategy, the larger scale plans of social movement actors. Tactics are selected from a larger repertoire or toolkit available for social movement groups (Swidler, 1986; Tilly, 2006). These toolkits are often inspired by past social movement campaigns (McAdam and Rucht, 1993) although groups sometimes innovate new tactics over time. The particular set of tactics that a group uses becomes its "claims-making routine" (Tilly, 1978, 2006).

There are a variety of tactics from which movement actors can select. Protest, such as hosting demonstrations in the street or marches, is the tactic most readily associated with modern social movements. Tarrow (2011, p. 100) tells us that "the organized public demonstration represents the main conventional expression of movement activity today." In fact, the wave of mobilization that spawned the Indivisible groups at the center of this study was sparked by a large demonstration, the Women's March on January 21, 2017.

Researchers have investigated the link between the use of particular tactics, particularly protest tactics, and outcomes for both individuals and groups. Klandermans (1993) finds that the choice of tactics had significant effects on the level of participation among the general Dutch population. He compares three events: a demonstration held by the peace movement, a strike waged by a labor union, and an attempt to mobilize women into community feminist groups by the women's movement. He finds that the demonstration was the most effective at mobilizing activists and the tactic of creating local group chapters was the least effective. It is also important to examine the effect of engaging in protest on individual trajectories of participation. Christens and Speer (2011) assess the role of protest participation in congregation-based community organizations and show that engaging in this tactic can have important effects on how individuals participate over time, keeping them active in the group. Both Klandermans's and Christens and Speer's works highlight the ways in which an organization's use of protest tactics can have important implications for their ability to mobilize members, and both projects highlight how effective protest, in particular, can be at mobilizing activists.

Despite the prominence of protest as a social movement tactic, it is certainly not the only tactic available to activists. Many social movement groups do not engage in protest activity, instead choosing a variety of noncontentious ways to gain attention for their issues. For example, social movements often engage in political activity aimed at electoral targets. Hosting town halls, lobbying elected officials, supporting electoral campaigns, and strategically registering voters are all tactics aimed at the electoral process. Earlier definitions of social movements focused, almost exclusively, on the ways that movement organizations worked outside of the traditional routes of political power. However, it is clear that social movement actors often engage in a combination of traditional and nontraditional routes to exert influence, and we miss some of their important work if we look only outside of electoral channels to understand their activities. Many social movement groups incorporate both of these types of tactics into their repertoires (Fisher, 2012; Goldstone, 2003; McAdam and Tarrow, 2010). For example, many of the Indivisible groups in this analysis hosted town halls aimed at pressuring their local elected officials to support the Affordable Care Act (ACA) and, in the lead-up to the midterm elections of 2018, many supported local candidates and went door-to-door to get out the vote.

Many modern movements also engage in a variety of activities outside of protest and electoral tactics. For example, people get together for film screenings and pub nights and to listen to speakers on a variety of topics. These activities are sometimes aimed at making social change outside of politics, such as in the cultural, economic, or religious spheres, and are sometimes focused on developing organizations. Reger and Staggenborg (2006) use the term "mobilizing tactic" to indicate a tactic chosen for its potential influence on recruitment and organizational maintenance. These types of tactics can be external, aimed at achieving movement goals, or internal, intended primarily to build organizations. They are conceptually important in generating collective action, maintaining organizations, and solidifying social ties and collective identities within groups (see McAdam, 1982; Schmitt and Martin, 1999; Voss and Sherman, 2000).

Empirical examinations of the effect of engaging in nonpolitical tactics have been less common in the literature. This is because most research on social movements has focused on groups that try to effect political change by targeting the state with contentious tactics (W. Gamson, 1975; Giugni, 1988; McAdam, 1982; McAdam, Tarrow, and Tilly, 2001). As a result, until the past few decades, research on social movements was not as attuned to how movements use nonpolitical tactics aimed at cultural change across multiple fields (Armstrong and Bernstein, 2008; Binder, 2002; Van Dyke, Soule, and Taylor, 2004).

The emerging work in this area focuses on the effect of engaging in mobilizing tactics aimed at building organizations on the longevity of groups. Reger and Staggenborg (2006) found that chapters of the National Organization for Women were more likely to maintain continuous activities over time when they built an organizational repertoire of mobilizing tactics and used external events for internal purposes as well as social-change strategies. When members met at a potluck dinner, for example, they shared stories and camaraderie that help support their long-term engagement and the vibrancy of the group as a whole.

Work in this area also investigates how movements can expand through nonoppositional, consensus-building tactics (Klandermans, 1988; McCarthy and Wolfson, 1992; Pellow, 1999). For example, research on religious movements finds that these groups often mobilize through unobtrusive political tactics that build on existing social structures, rather than through contentious tactics that challenge these structures. Tactics such as discursive politics, developing a state within a state, burrowing into targeted organizations, and assimilating into mainstream organizations have been very effective for religious movements in particular (Kucinskas, 2014). Movements have a wide range of tactics from which to choose and the selection of a particular tactic can have important consequences for group mobilization and survival.

Diversification or Specialization

Groups differ in the diversity of tactics they use. Some groups engage in a wide array of tactics while others become specialized in a small set (or singular) tactic. The extent to which tactical diversity or specialization is beneficial for social movements has been debated in the literature (see Edwards and Marullo, 1995; Reger and Staggenborg, 2006; Singh and Lumsden, 1990; for counterexamples, see W. Gamson, 1975; Olzak and Johnson, 2019). Conventional wisdom holds that diversity benefits SMOs and causes. Writing about the US Civil Rights Movement of the 1960s, Oberschall (1973, p. 230) argues that "the multiplicity of civil rights organizations using different styles of protest, appealing to different constituencies, mobilizing different social strata, and in vigorous competition with each other . . . resulted in a kind of dynamism and steady civil rights activity that a well-organized, hierarchically led, better financed mass organization might not have provided in these years." In general, research finds that diversity of tactics in a given population of SMOs tends to increase the size of the mobilized population, which in turn increases a movement's capacity for collective action (Morris, 1993). Bernstein (1997) found that identity movements, in particular, receive substantial rewards from diversification. She argues that a "celebration of differences" (or diversity) within these movements increases the numbers of potential supporters by offering a wider repertoire of goals and tactics, which enhances the movement's chances for success (1997, p. 544; see also J. Gamson, 1996; Minkoff, 1999). Cress and Snow (2000, p. 1096) agree and contend that "most social movement outcomes are probably obtained through multiple pathways rather than through one sure-fire pathway or set of conditions." Work on a variety of movements supports this finding. For example, Pousadela finds that the success of the women's movement for legal abortion in Uruguay was a result of the breadth of its repertoire of action, progressively expanded to include various (and sometimes innovative) strategies operating in both the realm of civil society and public opinion, and the sphere of political institutions and political representation (2016, p. 125).

The research on tactical diversity tends to highlight how social movements as a whole, across a variety of organizations, benefit from using a wider repertoire of tactics. It is less clear, however, what the benefits are of using a diversity of tactics within one organization. Specializing in a small number of tactics, or even using one tactic repeatedly, could have benefits. This focused strategy could help an organization to develop a strong identity in the eyes of members and the public. Because of this, organizations may benefit from using a small repertoire of tactics repeatedly in order to facilitate the development of a strong identity or "brand." This is particularly true for older organizations and those working within more crowded environments (Minkoff, 1999). The benefits and costs of using a diversity of tactics within one organization is a central focus of this chapter and will be examined in the Indivisible groups at the heart of this study.

Flexibility

Groups differ in the degree to which they are flexible, or willing to change their tactics. There are benefits and costs to changing tactics. We might expect that groups would find tactics that work and then keep using these same tactics over time. Tilly (1978) notes this propensity, which he calls the advantage of familiarity. He argues that tactics become easier to use with more practice, and, for this reason, movement actors may be reluctant to try new tactics, especially if they have been successful with the tactics they are already using.

Benefits could also be derived from changing tactics. Doug McAdam (1983) developed the concept of tactical innovation to highlight the importance of developing or borrowing new tactics over time. He argued that tactical innovation is critical to the success of movements because this innovation helps sustain interest and attention over time. For example, civil rights protesters in the United States in the 1950s and 1960s innovated new tactics, such as bus boycotts and sit-ins at segregated lunch counters (McAdam, 1996; Morris, 1984; Tarrow, 2011). Later research has shown that tactical innovation has been critical across movements and times. LGBTQ activists, for example, created new tactics such as the kiss-in and pride parades to attract the public's attention to their demands (Brickell, 2000). In general, research finds that innovation or flexibility is critical for movements and organizations, and that groups that adapt their tactics in response to changing conditions are much more likely to survive over time (Ganz, 2009; McCammon, 2003; Reger and Staggenborg, 2006).

As is the case for diversity of tactics, there are different forces that would seemingly encourage flexibility, on the one hand, and consistency, on the other. Flexibility, like diversity, could be useful as it enables groups to embrace changing political contexts, avoid member burnout, and engage a variety of different kinds of members. However, consistency, like specialization, also has certain advantages, such as being able to support a strong group identity and "brand" that could help recruit and retain members.

Factors Shaping Tactical Choices

Not all tactics are available to all groups at all times. There are a variety of factors that shape the tactical choices of SMOs, and there has been a small body of literature that empirically investigates the determinants of these choices (e.g., McAdam, 1983; Minkoff, 1999; Shapiro, 1985; Staggenborg, 1989). Research has found that there are both internal and external factors at play. Internally, identity, organizational structure, and resources can shape tactical choices. Externally, political context and opportunities can affect the tactical choices of social movement groups.

Characteristics of the movement as a whole and organizations in particular can be critical in shaping tactical decisions (Minkoff, 1999). The role of organizational factors is highlighted in Carmin and Balser's (2002) research on the tactical choices of Greenpeace and Friends of the Earth. They found that internal factors, particularly experience, core values, environmental philosophy, and political ideology, worked together to create distinct assessments about which tactics would be most effective. These internal features combine to create an organizational identity that shapes a group's tactical choices.

Elements of the organizational structure are also associated with tactical choices. In particular, when organizations are formalized, they tend to be less likely to use disruptive and contentious tactics and are more likely to rely on institutional approaches to change (Piven and Cloward, 1977; Staggenborg, 1988). Work in this area has argued that, once organizations are formalized, they are less likely to engage in tactics that ask for large-scale revolutionary change and work outside the political system. Instead, they tend to focus on more evolutionary change within the political system.

Resources also shape tactical choices, making certain tactics more attractive and available to organizations (Jenkins and Perrow, 1977; McCarthy, Britt, and Wolfson, 1991). SMOs require a wide variety of resources, and these resources can both enable and constrain action. For example, groups need money to pay for equipment such as a loudspeaker for an event or posterboards for signs. Groups that have more money are more easily able to organize events like town halls, which require renting a room. And organizations that have human resources, such as many members, can more easily organize large protest events. If a group has little money and few members, it is very difficult to mobilize a large march, even if it would like to. Resources are clearly required to facilitate a group's tactical choices.

In addition to internal factors, elements of the external environment can shape the tactics available, and attractive, to movement organizations. In particular, political opportunities shape the types of tactics that groups select. The core premise of political opportunity theory is that mobilization is likely when changes in the political climate make collective action more likely to succeed. Examples of such opportunities are increases in the level of elite receptivity to protesters or the restructuring of existing power relations (Jenkins, Jacobs, and Agnone, 2003; Kitschelt, 1986; Meyer, 2004; Tarrow, 2011). Scholars have also argued that political competitiveness, which might occur in highly contested elections or when there are divisions within elites, can create opportunities for excluded groups to mobilize (Jenkins et al., 2003; Soule and Olzak, 2004). These periods of political conflict or instability may signal the possibility of success to movement actors and offer a political opportunity to mobilize (Brockett, 1991; Tarrow, 2011). Within the context of this study, the 2018 midterm elections was an example of a highly motivating opportunity for many of the groups and was critical in shaping their tactical choices.

McCammon (2003) highlights the importance of political defeats as a predictor of when a movement will mobilize and use a new tactic. A significant political defeat can send the message to activists that current tactics are ineffective and new ones are needed, and thus a defeat, rather than an opportunity, could provide the impetus for a change in tactics. Her research on the suffragist movement illustrates this and shows that defeats may have intensified the suffragists' resolve and pushed them to search for new and more successful ways of mobilizing. This finding is supported by a variety of research across movements that shows how significant failures may compel movements to try new tactics (Beckwith, 2000; Meyer, 1999). In fact, the massive size of the first Women's March is an illustration of the mobilization potential of defeats as it was mobilized in response to the election of Donald Trump.

Political opportunities can affect when a group mobilizes as well as what types of tactics it will select. When opportunities are present and groups have more political access, movement actors typically rely on institutional avenues of influence (Tarrow, 2011; Tilly, 1978). When the political structure is relatively closed and difficult to penetrate, activists tend to adopt more expressive and unconventional tactical repertoires (Eisinger, 1973; Tarrow, 2011).

Examining the Role of Tactical Choices

This chapter focuses on how groups select their tactics and the effects of these decisions on groups over time. I focus on how groups select the *type*, *diversity*, and *flexibility* of tactics. By comparing across the thirty-five Indivisible groups in ten US cities, I am able to assess how internal organizational factors as well as external contextual conditions shape these decisions. And, in turn, I examine how group choices affect their ability to mobilize and survive over time. I began by examining the correlations between the types of tactics used, particularly the percentage of events that are protest or electorally focused, and group outcomes. I also examine the diversity of tactics (the number of distinct tactics used by the group) and if the group substantially changed their tactics from year 1 to year 2. Table 2.1 presents the correlations between these variables.

The correlations highlight the importance of tactical choice for both how much a group mobilizes and how likely it is to survive over time. Groups that protest more, as a percentage of all their activities, tend to mobilize more events over time (0.4594, p = 0.0063) and are more likely to survive (0.4102, p = 0.0160). Groups that engage in more electoral work, such as campaigning to elect a candidate or hosting town halls,

TABLE 2.1. Correlations between Tactics and Group Outcomes

	Protest (Percent)	Electoral (Percent)	Number of Tactics	Tactics Change	Number of Events	Survival
Protest (Percent)	—					
Electoral (Percent)	0.0875 (0.6227)	—				
Number of Tactics	0.1707 (0.3344)	0.4846 (0.0037)	—			
Tactics Change (1=Tactics Changed)	0.1161 (0.5133)	–0.0186 (0.9168)	0.3836 (0.0251)	—		
Number of Events	0.4594 (0.0063)	0.4035 (0.0180)	0.3450 (0.0457)	–0.3258 (0.0500)	—	
Survival	0.4102 (0.0160)	0.3985 (0.0196)	0.6539 (0.000)	0.1080 (0.5432)	0.5251 (0.0014)	—

also mobilize more events (0.4035, $p = 0.0180$) and are more likely to survive over time (0.3985, $p = 0.0196$). Using both of these types of political tactics is associated with positive outcomes and survival for groups.

Groups that engage in a diverse range of tactics mobilized more events (0.3450, $p = 0.0457$) and are more likely to survive over time (0.6539, $p = 0.000$). These are both quite strong and significant correlations, although the relationship between tactical diversity and survival is about twice as strong as the relationship between diversity and events. Being consistent in tactical choices over time is also associated with having more events (−0.3258, $p = 0.0500$) although it is not significantly correlated with group survival (0.1080, $p = 0.5432$).

One of the central arguments of this book is that similar strategies can have different effects depending on the local context. In order to examine this in more detail, I conducted a QCA. The QCA enables us to understand the multiple pathways to mobilization and survival in different contexts (Cress and Snow, 2000; Ragin, 1987). QCA techniques are based on Boolean logic (Ragin, 1987). They allow us to consider all possible combinations of theoretically proscribed causal factors and, with its comparative algorithmic logic, eliminate redundant and superfluous information. The benefits of the QCA lie in its ability to specify configurations of variables that shape outcomes. Table 2.2 presents the QCA findings. As is standard in presenting QCA results, capital letters indicate the presence of a condition and lowercase letters indicate its absence. An asterisk (*) indicates "and." The table also presents consistency and coverage, two key concepts in QCA. Consistency is the percentage of the causal configurations with the specific composition that results in the same outcome variable. Coverage is the number of cases for which the configuration is valid (Roig-Tierno, Gonzalez-Cruz, and Llopis-Martinez, 2017). (For more information on the QCA method and how it was used in these analyses, see the Methodological Appendix.)

The QCA indicates that there are three routes to having a large number of events, as shown in table 2.2. I coded groups that had more than thirty-six events as having a "high" number of events. This would mean that groups had, on average, at least 1.5 events per month over the two years. In reality, all the groups coded as "low events" had nineteen or fewer events in total, and there were no groups that had between twenty and thirty-five events in the two-year period. This made the cutoff of thirty-six both theoretically and empirically useful. The first route to a high number of events involved the combination of using a large amount of protest and electoral work and a diversity of tactics (Political, Diverse).[1] This was the most common route to having a high number of events, with 58 percent raw coverage and 26 percent unique coverage. Second, groups could engage in a large amount of protest and a diversity of tactics but keep their tactics consistent over time (Protest, Diverse, Consistent). This was the second most common route with 42 percent coverage and 11 percent unique coverage. Finally, groups could engage in high levels of protest and electoral work and not change their tactics over time (Political, Consistent). This route had 37 percent coverage and 5 percent unique coverage.

There were also three routes to group survival (see table 2.3).[2] These different routes account, in part, for the lack of statistical significance in the relationship between tactical consistency and group survival. First, groups could engage in a large amount of protest and a diversity

TABLE 2.2. QCA Results for Number of Events

EVENTS		Raw Coverage	Unique Coverage	Consistency	Groups
PROTEST* ELECTORAL* NUMBERTACTICS	Political, Diverse	0.579	0.263 (Pittsburgh 3; Amarillo 1; SLC 2, 3; Pasadena 1)	0.917	Atlanta 1, 3, 5, 6; Pittsburgh 3; Amarillo 1; SLC 2, 3; Pasadena 1; Portland 6, 7;
PROTEST* NUMBERTACTICS* TacticsChange	Protest, Diverse, Consistent	0.421	0.105 (Pittsburgh 5; Bridgeport 1)	0.801	Atlanta 1, 3, 5, 6; Portland 6, 7; Pittsburgh 5; Bridgeport 1
PROTEST* ELECTORAL* *TacticsChange	Political, Consistent	0.368	0.052 (Atlanta 4)	0.875	Dayton 1; Atlanta 1, 3, 4, 5, 6; Portland 6, 7

Solution coverage = 0.737; solution consistency = 0.875.
Uppercase letters indicate the presence of a condition and lowercase letters indicate its absence. An asterisk (*) indicates "and." The table also presents consistency and coverage, two key concepts in the QCA. Consistency is the percentage of the causal configurations with the specific composition that results in the same outcome variable. Coverage is the number of cases for which the configuration is valid (Roig-Tierno, Gonzalez-Cruz, and Llopis-Martinez, 2017).

TABLE 2.3. QCA Results for Group Survival

SURVIVAL		Raw Coverage	Unique Coverage	Consistency	Groups
PROTEST* NUMBERTACTICS	Protest, Diverse	0.739	0.130 (Springfield 1; Pittsburgh 5; Bridgeport 1)	0.944	Dayton 1; Springfield 1, 2; Pittsburgh 3, 4, 5; Pasadena 1; Bridgeport 1; Atlanta 1, 3, 5, 6; Amarillo 1; Portland 6, 7; SLC 2, 3
NUMBERTACTICS* TACTICSCHANGE	Diverse, Flexible	0.434	0.130 (Pasadena 2; Amarillo 2; SLC 1)	0.910	Springfield 2; Pittsburgh 3, 4; Pasadena 1, 2; Amarillo 1, 2; SLC 1, 2, 3
PROTEST* ELECTORAL* *TacticChange	Political, Focused, Consistent	0.347	0.043 (Atlanta 4)	1	Dayton 1; Atlanta 1, 3, 4, 5, 6; Portland 6, 7

Solution coverage = 0.9130; solution consistency = 0.9545.
Uppercase letters indicate the presence of a condition and lowercase letters indicate its absence. An asterisk (*) indicates "and." The table also presents consistency, the percentage of the causal configurations with the specific composition that results in the same outcome variable, and coverage, the number of cases for which the configuration is valid.

of tactics (Protest, Diverse).[3] This was the most common route and had 74 percent coverage with 13 percent unique coverage. The second route involved using a diversity of tactics and changing those tactics over time (Diverse, Flexible). This route had 43 percent coverage and 13 percent unique coverage. Finally, groups could engage in high levels of protest and electoral work and also be consistent in their tactics over time (Political, Focused, Consistent). This route was also present in the QCA explaining group events over time. This route accounted for 35 percent of the coverage in the events model and 4 percent of the unique coverage.

The Importance of Tactical Diversity

Engaging in a diversity of tactics is an important part of how groups are able to mobilize a large number of events and survive over time. The statistical analysis shows a strong and positive relationship between engaging in a diversity of tactics, on the one hand, and hosting a large number of events and surviving, on the other hand. In predicting events, using a diversity of tactics was a component of two of the routes that had 42 percent and 58 percent coverage, respectively (and 36 percent unique coverage combined). When looking at survival over time, two of the routes to survival involved using a diversity of tactics. One of these routes accounted for 74 percent of the coverage while the other accounted for 44 percent of the coverage (and 26 percent unique coverage combined). This diversity was also often paired with the use of protest tactics in the most common route for survival and in both routes for events.[4]

Pasadena 1, Amarillo 1, and Bridgeport 1 all had many events and survived the first two years of mobilization. All these groups engaged in a diversity of tactics and high levels of protest. However, they differed in their use of electoral tactics and their propensity to change tactics over time. Pasadena 1 and Amarillo 1 hosted many events through the Political, Diverse route (high protest, high electoral, many tactics) and survived over time through the Protest, Diverse route (high levels of protest, many tactics). Bridgeport 1 hosted many events through the Diverse, Consistent route (many tactics, little change over time) and survived through the Protest, Diverse route (high protest, many tactics). They have in common their use of protest and a diversity of tactics, but other decisions differed. Let's consider each of these group contexts in more detail.

Pasadena 1 hosted many events (180 events in the first year) and survived until the end of year 2. Its events were highly varied. This was mostly due to internal factors, including the needs of its members and the group's organizational structure. These two internal factors shaped the broad tactical repertoire used by Pasadena 1.

The tactics of Pasadena 1 were selected to facilitate the engagement of group members. Like many of the Indivisible groups, Pasadena 1 began by hosting mostly protest events, such as the original Women's March and a series of protests focused on local policing and access to clean water. As Alice describes, "There were lots of protests here at Pasadena City Hall because there seems to be, everywhere in the US, problems with police overstepping their bounds and killing people. So that was something we really wanted to do."

Over time, the Pasadena 1 activists incorporated electoral tactics, particularly a series of town halls aimed at swaying elected representatives. These town halls were very well organized. The group leaders invited elected officials to answer questions about the repeal of the ACA. Members would prearrange to sit together in small groups distributed around the room. This served the dual purpose of providing solidarity to members who were to ask questions, which could be quite stressful, while also bolstering the impression that there were a variety of different constituent groups who were interested in these issues. The group distributed a list of potential questions that members could ask the elected officials. They divided the questions so that all the key topics were covered. This ensured that members felt confident and comfortable asking questions, as they were well prepared, and also that the elected officials would have to respond to a variety of topic areas. The members also all agreed that, if the elected leader attempted to evade the question, the next group member would ask the same question until it was answered.

The town halls were initially quite successful. However, for practical reasons, they were difficult for the group to sustain. The group mostly targeted representatives who were not local and, as a result, these events were far from the Pasadena area and members found it difficult to travel long distances to participate in them. The town halls did continue, but they were no longer run by Pasadena 1. And, while some members still engaged in them, they were no longer a core tactic of the group as a whole.

The group's flexible and inclusive structure also led to the use of a diversity of tactics. This was also the result of a larger strategy in the group to work to integrate its members. One way it did this was by intentionally working to provide venues where members could introduce and lead campaigns. As Alice explains,

> When you came to the meetings, we would run through the preliminary stuff and then we would break up into groups. And so, if someone asked to speak and said "I really want to create a group that's around reproductive rights and I'll be over here in that part of the room when we break up," then anyone who was interested could go and join them. And maybe that group would organize a protest. And another group would say they were interested in health care and they would organize a town hall.

Because the group actively worked to bring in many activists to plan events, there was always a diversity of types of issues and events on the agenda. In this way, the nonhierarchical structure of the group shaped the number and diversity of tactics that the group used.

This more inclusive strategy had both benefits and costs. The most notable benefits were that the diversity of leaders and campaigns fostered vibrancy in the group, facilitated the ongoing participation of members over time, and increased the mobilization potential of the group as a whole. However, there were also costs to this strategy. First, because not all of the members who suggested campaigns were experienced activists or had the time and energy to follow through on their plans, not all of the issue groups were able to effectively launch actions. In addition, the inclusive style and wider group of issue leaders in Pasadena 1 led to somewhat less coherence in the overall agenda of the group. Smaller subgroups were organizing town halls on health care, postcard campaigns on voter registration, and protests about reproductive rights. This was attractive for group members who were interested in different causes but could have a negative effect on the long-term cohesion of the group as these smaller subgroups did not often overlap and cross-fertilize.

Bridgeport 1 also hosted many events and survived through year 2. And, like Pasadena 1 and Amarillo 1, discussed earlier in the chapter, it also engaged in a wide diversity of tactics. However, Bridgeport 1 came to embrace this diversity as a result of two external factors. First, the leaders of Bridgeport 1 were very focused on building activist networks, which involved cooperating with a wide range of groups who engaged in a diversity of tactics. Second, the leaders of Bridgeport 1 were very reactive to the local political and activist context.

Bridgeport 1 was notable in the massive number of events listed on its page, with 619 events listed in two years, and often multiple events listed on one day. This large number of events was the result of extensive cooperation between Bridgeport 1 and other local groups. There was a very high level of cross-listing of events and coalition work (discussed in more detail in chapter 3). Bridgeport 1 engaged in a wide range of tactics. In the early months, it particularly focused on protests, such as the rally against the Muslim ban, the People's Climate March, and the Vigil for Charlottesville. It also hosted many organizational meetings, social events, and rallies with local political candidates. These events were interspersed so that many weeks would have electoral events, protests, social gatherings, and organizational meetings.

The group focused on connecting with other local organizations. As Susan describes, the group was "trying to build a network across different organizations." And, because the group was so focused on creating these network ties, it tended to be more responsive to what other groups were doing. As Linda explains, the group was reactive in two main ways.

[First,] a couple of our organizers have formed with a bunch of other women this Connecticut Black Women's Group. So, if they ask us to show up at a rally, we're going to show up. That wasn't our idea to do that, but we're not going to say no. The same with, we're now part of the Reproductive Rights Coalition in Connecticut. We're not leading it, it's being led by Pro-Choice Connecticut and Planned Parenthood Connecticut. Again, whatever they ask us, they say, "We're having a phone bank, can you guys help with turnout? We're having a rally, can you guys help with turnout?" We're going to say yes, of course. That gets added to our list of things to do, even if it wasn't on our agenda initially.

The group was also very reactive to the national Indivisible organization, something that was surprisingly uncommon among the Indivisible groups in this study. While all the groups were initially inspired by Indivisible, as indicated by their decision to be listed on the Indivisible website, Bridgeport 1 was one of only two groups in this study that explicitly mentioned responding to calls to action from the national organization over time.[5] Linda describes how, in the first year, the national Indivisible group would say:

"Okay, in two weeks we're doing A Day without a Woman, go." What, in two weeks? Also, we don't agree with the idea of A Day without a Woman, and we got no input, and now it's been announced nationally so we're getting flooded with people asking us questions about it. We were constantly scrambling to respond to what they were putting out as a national call to action.

In general, Linda explains, "We still are in a lot of ways just putting ourselves at use to whoever's asking us to be of use and that means spreading ourselves in lots of different ways because we just don't say no as long as it comports with our principles." Despite the pressure that this put on the group, the members were able to create strong connections with other local organizations and, as a result, hosted or cohosted a very large number of events and stayed active over time.

Comparing the trajectories of these three groups, we can see that Pasadena 1 and Amarillo 1 embraced a diversity of tactics because of internal organizational structures and decisions to include a diversity of members while organizing. Bridgeport 1 came to use a diversity of tactics as a result of their engagement with other groups. Despite these different reasons for embracing tactical diversity, all three of these groups benefited from engaging in a wide range of tactics over time.

The (Varying) Importance of Flexibility

The relationship between tactical flexibility and group outcomes is complex. Changing tactics over time was statistically significantly related to the number of events a group hosted. The more a group changed their tactics over time, the fewer events it hosted on average. In this way, having a consistent tactic (or set of tactics) was positive for mobilizing. As discussed, groups benefited from having a diversity of tactics, but these tactical repertoires should be consistent over time.

Consistency often occurred in combination with the use of political tactics. Many groups that engaged in political tactics became committed to them over time. There were a number of reasons for this. First, members enjoyed these tactics and felt emotionally supported by other members when participating in them, making them popular within the groups. Second, group members often described how engaging in protest, in particular, was important for providing a face to activism in the community. Finally, groups that engaged in protest consistently developed particular types of organizational identities and, as a result, felt committed to the tactics that supported these identities in the eyes of their members, the public, and the media.

There are many factors that can influence a group's choice of tactic. However, one consideration must be to select a tactic that group members enjoy. This helps encourage both initial participation and keeps members active over time. Protest was clearly a tactic that many group members enjoyed. Statistical analysis shows that engagement in a high level of protest was associated with more group events and survival over time. In addition, protest was an important condition in all three routes to having a high number of events and in two of the three routes to group survival. It was not a necessary condition, however, because it was not present in three cases where groups did host many events but did not fit into any of the routes in the QCA.

Many group members talked about how much they enjoyed engaging in protest. Simply put, as Julia explains, "It's fun to go to a rally" (Dayton 1). And protests help to create feelings of solidarity and efficacy. Steve, a member of Pasadena 1, describes this:

> Protests are fun for sure. And they're energizing and there's great value to that. We did a protest down at one of the detention centers downtown for undocumented people who are facing possible deportation. And just being there with all these other groups like ICE out of LA, and CHIRLA, groups that do way, way, way more work than we do on immigration, but we can be there to help. And little things like hearing the prisoners inside, clicking on their windows to signal that they knew we were out there and that they heard, that was like something that you can't even put into words as far as just how much that means in a way that really isn't measurable.

The feeling of being with one's fellow activists and interacting with the public or constituents, like the undocumented people whom Steve's group was trying to help, was empowering and inspired further commitment to protest as a tactic in the group as a whole.

Protest also served important functions beyond the group. Activists felt that visible events, particularly protests, were important because they sent signals to the local community, potential recruits, and the media. Protest highlights the existence of a group of people who oppose Trump or support specific progressive policies. This was particularly important in areas where there were smaller progressive communities. As Debbie from Pittsburgh 4 explains, "We were protesting and we realized that this performance was a self-affirmation and it became very important as a social construct for those drivers to realize that people of all ages and all colors were out there and they weren't happy with the direction of the country. It was social affirmation that they weren't alone." Protest also could work to change the opinions of the public. Nancy, from Pittsburgh 3, noted this critical role of protest: "The protests are so important, I feel. Not that things change as a result of a protest, but it lets people know that right here in your local community there are people who are concerned and have issues with things that are going on. And that influences people." From this perspective, it made sense to continue the protests even when they were not perceived as effective at changing policy.

Tactical choices are also related to group identity. Many groups came to strongly identify with one particular tactic over time, making it less likely that they would change tactics even if their current approach did not seem to be effective. For example, Dayton 1 consistently engaged in protest tactics over time, even though leaders in the group acknowledged that the protests may not have been making much of a difference in the local political landscape. Almost all of these protest events were focused on feminist issues, the core concern of the group. Dayton 1 had been an activist organization for almost twenty-five years prior to the first Women's March. As Julia explains, the group "came out of the women's liberation movement" and had existed long before Indivisible started organizing. It has been engaging in the same sorts of tactics and campaigns for its entire twenty-five-year history, all protest centered and focused on feminist issues. However, before the first Women's March, the group attracted only small groups of five or six people to protest events. When the group participated in the first local Women's March, group members were surprised and pleased with the turnout of fifty to sixty people. After the march, the group signed up on the Indivisible website in the hopes of attracting more people to its cause. And it worked. The group started to bring 200 people to its regular protests and was able to mobilize about 3,000 people to the second Women's March in Dayton.

The case of Dayton 1 highlights a few key things about the role of group identity in tactical choices. First, the group engaged in protest as a tactic because of its overarching identity as an "activisty" group, as described by Julia. It did not matter if the contexts changed: engaging in feminist protest is part of who group members are, and so this is what they did, regardless of changing circumstances. Second, the founding of Indivisible brought more people to this preexisting group but, interestingly, did not change the group. The group continued with its tactics and simply incorporated the new members. In this way, we would expect that, even after Indivisible stops organizing groups online (if this happens), the group would presumably continue to mobilize, as its origin predated Indivisible as an organizing structure.

The importance of protest for group survival is evident in both the correlational analysis and the QCA. It is clear that protest serves a number of important functions for groups. And, while it was possible to mobilize without it, it was much more difficult. Protest had important internal functions, working to energize the group and maintain commitment over time. Groups did not have to protest consistently or as their only tactic. However, having protest as part of a group's repertoire allowed it to reap these benefits. Protests were also effective ways to mobilize new members and attract attention from outsiders. Without any protest events, groups risked becoming insular, which made survival over time a challenge.

Changing tactics over time was not statistically significantly related to group survival. However, the QCA shines light on why this is the case. There were two different routes to group survival that involved tactical change over time. In one route, staying consistent in tactics over time (when used in combination with high levels of electoral and protest tactics) was linked to group survival. This is the same combination of factors that also predicted a high number of events. However, there was another route where changing tactics over time (in combination with using a diversity of tactics) was linked to group survival. This analysis makes clear that changing tactics over time is sometimes good and sometimes not, depending on the combination of other factors that come with this flexibility.

The organizers for Salt Lake City 3 were very flexible in their tactics and were successful in mobilizing and surviving over time. There were three main factors that led the group to use a diversity of tactics and be flexible in the use of these tactics. First, the group regularly assessed the effectiveness of its tactics over time and then updated tactical choices. Second, the group responded quickly to larger changes in the political environment, both locally and nationally. And, finally, the leaders were concerned about the burnout of members and wanted to provide variety and diversity in engagement over time to keep members active and satisfied with their participation.

Salt Lake City 3 was a very successful group, hosting 182 events and surviving until the second anniversary march. One of the main reasons for this was that the group constantly assessed tactics and altered them to increase efficacy. This was quite unusual. As the example of Dayton 1, discussed earlier, illustrates, groups often remained consistent in their tactics over time, even when these tactics were not very effective. This was frequently because they felt committed to these tactics because of the identity of the group. However, it is also a result of the fact that some groups were not always very reflective about how changing contexts might make a tactic less effective over time. Research on other movements also highlights how groups are not always accurate in assessing the efficacy of their tactics (Blee, 2012; Lichterman, 2005). This makes the very reflective and flexible tactics of Salt Lake City 3 all the more notable.

Salt Lake City 3 began by engaging in tactics focused on trying to pressure current local elected leaders to change their votes on issues such as the ACA. As Stefanie explains, "The whole first year was like that, just demonstrations constantly and at our members of Congress all the time." However, starting in 2018, organizers in the groups started to reassess this plan. The group debated in long meetings over coffee in one of the leaders' living rooms about how it could change tactics to be more effective. It became clear that the elected leaders in their area were very unlikely to be swayed into voting against the interests of President Trump on most legislation. "At the end of the first year, we realized that our members of Congress are not movable. Mike Lee, one of our senators is, he's to the right of Attila the Hun. He wasn't going to be on the ballot, he's got four more years. You can't budge him. Orrin Hatch was senile, and he was headed towards retirement anyway. So that was hopeless" (Stefanie, Salt Lake City 3). Recognizing that the original tactic of lobbying was ineffective given the local context, the group decided to change tactics and focus on electing new political leaders in the 2018 midterm elections.

The group reasoned that, in order to elect new leaders, it had to increase voter turnout in the area. Utah has relatively low voter turnout, and the group decided that increasing voter registration would be a strategic way to reach its policy goals. As Stefanie explains, "We started between March and August. We had three voter registration trainings, and we trained about 140 people, plus we had a lot of people who learned on the job." This group of volunteers then began registering new voters for the upcoming midterm elections.

The group was also strategic in its decision of who and where to register voters, and this targeting was increasingly focused over time. First, it registered young people in high schools and universities. As Michael describes, "We're not partisans, so we register anyone. But, we knew that young voters would overwhelmingly, by a margin of like nine to one, vote for the Democrat. So, we were trying to get demographics that would vote against [Mia Love]." Salt Lake City 3 partnered with a local nonpartisan group called Voterize. As Stefanie explains:

At first, we had Voterize set the agenda, what high schools we were going to go to, and then we thought, no, we have a goal here. We're focused on national elections and we want to be effective. If we just go to the places they want us to go to, maybe we'll end up registering a couple thousand people in the four different congressional districts, but that's not strategic. Because one of those districts we're satisfied with. We felt like we had the best Republican in there we could get and so we didn't want to waste our time there. The other two districts, one is totally noncompetitive and then there's a big one, it's Salt Lake but then it runs all the way down to the southern part of the state, more than 250 miles south of here. It's totally gerrymandered. We had a good Democratic candidate but in that district the incumbent could lose every vote in Salt Lake County, which is the liberal part, and still win. It's so gerrymandered it's really impossible for a Democrat there. That left us with this Mia Love/Ben McAdams CD4 [Fourth Congressional District], which really was competitive. We thought, you know what? We'll work with Voterize but we want to set our own agenda, so we identified all the high schools in CD4 and said we'll do high school registration but we want to do it in these schools, not in the schools that you're directing us to. And they said, "Fine, that's great. We'll send other people to those other school districts." We had a couple of people calling the school districts to set up the schedule, and for most of April and May we had people every lunch hour, three or four people every lunch hour at high schools preregistering kids.

Voter registration was also an effective tactic because it appears nonpartisan to outsiders. The overall civic good of registering voters is generally seen as a positive thing, even within conservative contexts. This was particularly important in an area like Salt Lake City, where there was a more negative reception to activities that were seen as explicitly progressive and political. Framing voter registration as nonpartisan allowed the group access to many places where it could register voters without calling attention to the underlying political intention of its actions and eliciting repression. The group went into many high schools and universities in the area. Michael describes how access was quite easy in the first year. The principals let the Indivisible group into the schools, and volunteers were allowed to freely walk the lunchrooms. The plan was that "you go up to a table and you ask one person and if the first person says yes, then everybody will do it." Over time, however, once the group was becoming more successful at registering students, principals became increasingly hesitant to let the volunteers into the schools. And, even when they were allowed in, the volunteers were restricted in what they could do. As Michael explains, "So now they say 'you have to sit at your table.' And really that was a bomb after that. No high school kid is going to come up to our table, so we just sat there alone, registering no one."

The voter registration tactic was very effective in the early months. The group estimates that about 180 to 200 volunteers worked to register new voters through Salt Lake City 3. A core group of about twenty-five to thirty members was particularly active, volunteering once a week or more. By the end of this campaign, the group had registered almost 13,000 new voters in Utah's Fourth Congressional District. And, Mia Love, the incumbent Republican, lost the midterm election by 700 votes. This success was very motivating for the group and spurred on continued engagement.

Salt Lake City 3 also engaged in a diversity of tactics and changed its tactics over time in response to changing political opportunities. One larger political shift that altered its tactics was the midterm elections of 2018. After the election, it was more difficult to get members interested in voter registration, which now felt less immediately relevant. Just as the group used the upcoming midterms to refresh tactics and move from lobbying to voter registration, the passing of the midterm elections encouraged the group to again reconsider tactics.

Another political opportunity for mobilization emerged after Donald Trump visited Utah in December 2017. On this visit, he signed a proclamation to reduce the size of the Bear Ears and Grand Staircase Escalante national monuments from 1.35 million acres to 201,876 acres. This smaller area was made into two new monuments: Shash Jaa and Indian Creek (Davidson and Burr, 2017). These areas were no longer protected as national monuments, and this opened up the possibility of mining and drilling on the land. The changes to Bear Ears and Grand Staircase Escalante were highlighted by Trump's visit and the following two years, during which local conservationist, tribal, and paleontology groups engaged in a court challenge of this change in designation. The issue remained on the agenda well into 2020, when Trump finalized plans to allow mining and drilling on this land. These decisions changed the local activist context and were very effective issues around which to mobilize. Like voter registration, protecting the local natural monuments was almost a consensus issue and could easily be framed in a nonpolitical way. This was particularly important in the conservative context of Salt Lake City where the group was organizing.

Engaging in a variety of tactics and changing those tactics over time were also critical for helping members avoid burnout and continue to enjoy participating in the group. The early lobbying work was often unsatisfying for group members. It was difficult to see the tangible results of the actions, and volunteers became frustrated. The voter registration was a more positive experience for members. They participated in groups and it was a social experience. There was also an obvious and tangible result to their work each day—a list of ten or twenty newly registered voters. As Stefanie explains:

> It turned out that people loved doing [voter registration]. Everybody was burned out on calling our representatives. It was so negative, and it just wasn't getting us anywhere. But it turns out that registering people, whether or not the outcome of the election is what you want, is a very positive, proactive thing for people to do because it's getting more people engaged in our democratic process. People really glommed onto it, and they enjoyed doing it. I said to somebody, it's like washing the kitchen floor. You wash the kitchen floor, and you look at it and you think, "I have a clean floor." There's something just fundamentally satisfying about that even if you didn't really want to do it in the first place. If you go out and you come home with ten registrations in your hand, you feel like you've accomplished something.

Voter registration was empowering and helped members deal with the frustrations they felt with the current political context in their local area.

Pittsburgh 3 was also flexible in changing its tactics over time, and there was a sharp change in tactics between year 1 and year 2. The group spent the first year engaging in intensive community building through a series of potlucks and other social events. Pittsburgh 3 was particularly concerned with proposed changes to the ACA and climate change. In order to address these issues, group members engaged in lobbying, particularly letter-writing campaigns and calling local elected leaders. As Nancy explains, these tactics were selected to make the most of the resources the group members already brought to the table. They were mostly urban, professional, middle-class women. Because of this background, they had strong communication skills and were adept at organizing these types of campaigns. They also tended to feel comfortable writing letters and calling officials because of their professional and educational backgrounds as lawyers, social workers, and journalists.

The Pittsburgh 3 campaigns were very successful at mobilizing members. Organizers estimate that the group attracted almost 7,000 people in the first three months. Weekly meetings usually brought together at least twenty members, with some meetings attracting forty people. Despite the high mobilization in this group, activists began to feel disenchanted with the efficacy of their tactics. As Nancy explains:

> Calling elected leaders was our focus for about a year, until frankly we realized nobody was listening to us. That's what it felt like anyway. We have one Democratic congressman here who is already good. Then we have a Republican senator who doesn't give a crap what we think. It just sort of ended up feeling like we ought to shift to getting different people in office, because we're not making any inroads.

While their tactics had been effective at mobilizing members, it was deemed unlikely to change policy outcomes. As a result, in the second year, the group moved to mobilizing around electing Conor Lamb to

Congress in a special election in March 2018 against Republican Rick Saccone. Group members volunteered to canvas for Lamb, particularly in rural areas outside of the city core where his support was weaker. They also adapted their letter-writing campaign, moving away from in-person events to writing letters online.

Both Salt Lake City 1 and Pittsburgh 3 were notable in how adept they were at assessing the efficacy of their tactics. Both groups were able to mobilize many people early with their initial tactical choice of lobbying local officials. However, both groups were working within contexts where these local officials were not very responsive to their tactics and did not seem likely to change their policies. This led to high levels of frustration among the members of both groups about the perceived ineffectiveness of the tactics. While this could have led to demobilization or high levels of individual drop out, both groups were able to redirect the work of their members through strategic changes in tactics. This was made possible because both groups had regular vibrant meetings where a small group of skilled leaders worked to harness frustration and offer pathways forward, in the form of focusing on the 2018 midterm elections. The skill of the leadership groups and the role of regular meetings were both critical to enabling these groups to avoid the pitfalls of demobilization and group decline.

The Political, Consistent route was much more common in the larger cities (seven out of eight of the groups that followed the route involving tactical consistency were in large cities) and in more liberal areas (all the groups that followed this route were in more liberal areas). This could be because larger cities and areas that are more liberal tend to have a larger social movement sector. This allows for more specialization in the sector and encourages groups to select their tactics and commit to them. In smaller cities, especially those without long histories of activism, groups that survived were more often engaged in a more flexible repertoire of tactics (eight out of ten of the groups that survived using flexible tactics were in small cities). The cities using this more flexible route were also more likely to be in conservative areas (seven out of ten of the groups in the flexible route were in conservative areas). The groups in these smaller cities were more agile in changing their tactics over time to appeal to diverse crowds and normalize activism.[6] Salt Lake City 3, in particular, illustrates how flexibility can work very effectively in a smaller and more conservative city context.

Conclusion: The Role of Tactics

Activists make many important decisions as they organize. One of the most important decisions is the selection of which tactics to use. There are many internal and external factors that shape which tactics are available and attractive to a group. Additionally, there are many conditions that facilitate, or limit, the efficacy of the tactics once used.

Activists looking for guidance in selecting the most effective tactic will find some useful information in the experiences of the Indivisible groups at the heart of this study. Clearly there are some tactics that are very effective for helping groups mobilize and survive over time. The statistical analysis and QCA results both show the importance of engaging in protest and electoral tactics. Engagement in protest was important for a variety of reasons. First, it was simply an enjoyable tactic for many of the groups in this study. As activist Saul Alinsky famously said in his 1971 book, *Rules for Radicals*, a good tactic is one that your people enjoy. When members enjoy a tactic, they are more likely to keep coming back week after week, sustaining their individual engagement and the group over time. Protest was also an important way that group members sent signals to their community. Many activists want others in their area to know that there are progressive people among them, that opposition to Trump and his policies is vibrant, and that activism is a normal part of their community.

Electoral work was also associated with having more events and group survival. The timeline of this study spanned the period leading up to and just after the 2018 midterm elections. These elections saw a very high level of engagement and voting, relative to other midterm elections.

In fact, the voter turnout in the 2018 midterms was the highest for a midterm election since 1914. It was also a very successful election for Democrats, with the party gaining a net total of forty-one seats and winning a majority in the House of Representatives. All of these conditions help explain the relative importance of electoral tactics in this period. Groups active in organizing for this election were doing so within a context characterized by high levels of interest, engagement, and potential efficacy. The successes that many of these groups experienced in these campaigns helped to motivate them to continue to mobilize even after the 2018 midterm elections were over.

This chapter also highlights how it is not simply the type of tactic that is important. Any one tactic alone is not as effective as embracing a diversity of tactics. Some groups were structured in a way that made embracing a diverse tactical repertoire more likely. In particular, groups that were nonhierarchical were particularly receptive to engaging in a diversity of tactics. This is because they allowed a variety of group members to organize campaigns, leading to a wider range of tactics being undertaken within the group. An additional benefit of empowering members to lead campaigns is that it helps keep members active and invested over time and supports the long-term survival of the group.

Groups that engaged actively in coalitions with other groups also tended to embrace a diversity of tactics. This is because, when groups partner with other organizations, they are often at least somewhat open to the different tactics that the various groups bring to the table. This encouraged groups to embrace a diverse set of tactics. The importance of coalitions is examined in more detail in the next chapter.

In general, being consistent in tactics was good for groups. When groups were consistent, particularly in combination with using protest, they were much more likely to host a high number of events over time. The relationship between consistency and group survival was more complex. In some situations, being consistent was an important condition for survival, again when used with political tactics such as protest. In other situations, being flexible was very effective, especially when used in combination with a diversity of tactics. This route to survival was particularly common in smaller cities and conservative areas. The differing role of consistency and flexibility is highlighted by the QCA, which allows us to see the multiple pathways to survival for groups. This also highlights the ways that local context shape how groups select tactics and the impact of these tactics on group survival over time.

3

Creating a Vibrant Civil Society

Coalition Strategies and Movement Success

The first Women's March in 2017 was a coalition affair. It brought together activists focused on a wide variety of issues from women's rights to LGBTQ+ issues, Black Lives Matter (BLM), immigration, health care, the environment, and more. Social movement scholars have long known that coalitions can be a very successful tactic for social movements. When groups come together to share resources and coordinate actions, they can increase their voice and efficacy. The use of coalitions is clearly powerful, but how do groups enact this strategy and why is it so effective?

The Indivisible groups in the city of Bridgeport illustrate the importance of coalitions for SMOs. Bridgeport, the largest city in Connecticut with a population near 150,000, was the home of two Indivisible groups. These two groups took very different approaches to cooperating with other organizations. While Bridgeport 1 engaged in very high rates of coalition work, cooperating in almost all their events (92 percent), Bridgeport 2 was much more sparing in its collaborations, only cooperating about one-third of the time (35 percent). While both groups survived until the end of year 2, they had very different levels of mobilization. The coalition-focused group hosted 619 events in these two years while the group that worked more often in isolation hosted only seventeen events. How did Bridgeport 1 come to engage in such extensive coalition work and how did this facilitate their mobilization?

From the very founding of Bridgeport 1, there was a deep commitment to engaging in extensive coalition work. The founders of this group began discussing cooperating with other groups on the bus ride home from the first Women's March. They knew that the activists on the bus and those they had seen that day at the march were a powerful force. However, they did not want to usurp the activism of other groups who had been working on the ground in Connecticut for many years. Instead, they sought to harness their newfound enthusiasm to amplify the voices of others.

In the days and weeks following the march, activists in Bridgeport 1 started to reach out to local groups working on immigration reform, BLM, and LGBTQ+ issues in the state. As Linda describes, "We felt like there were groups in Connecticut that had been doing the boots-on-the-ground work for many, many years without much support or attention. Our thought was we have these 10,000 people in Hartford and a couple thousand that went to DC, a captive audience. Our role ought to be to let them know how to engage with groups that already exist. Funneling people to other groups." Bridgeport 1 wanted to "convert newly engaged volunteers into valuable resources for the groups here in Connecticut who were already mobilizing" by "connect[ing] newly energized volunteers to groups that had years and years of experience doing the work in the right way" (Linda, Bridgeport 1).

The activists in Bridgeport were very focused on avoiding even accidentally usurping groups that they felt better represented particular issue areas. As Linda explains,

> We work with the groups working on immigration reform that are immigrant led, and groups working on racial equality that are led by Black Lives Matter and those groups in the state. That has taken a couple of different forms. A lot of it means us just learning what's helpful to them and trying to shuttle what's helpful to them. Sometimes that's turnout for their events, sometimes that's connecting them to experts or legislators. Much of the time it's just following their lead, whatever they tell us to do, we do.

Bridgeport 1 fostered and sustained the coalition ties by pairing up one of their organizers with each local group with whom they worked. Linda describes how this tactic worked:

> We divvied up based on issues and said that each of us would commit to really becoming a committed supporter of the groups working on those issues and really try to form, as much as we could, authentic relationships in which we didn't just say . . . "Here's fifty middle-class white women who are do-gooders who've never done any kind of hard work before, here you go, do what you want with them." Because that wasn't necessarily so helpful.

The Indivisible activists were very responsive to the needs of their coalition partners and changed their tactics over time based on feedback from these local groups. In the first year, they invited two or three speakers on a variety of topics and asked them to talk about those topics. By the second year, they began

> reach[ing] out to the groups we've been working with and we would say, "You pick the speakers. You have fifteen minutes to talk about disability rights," or, "fifteen minutes to talk about racial justice," or, "fifteen minutes to talk about whatever. Tell us who you want to speak," or . . . we did workers' rights, we reached out to the unions and they decided to have a union chorus singing group. It was actually fabulous and picked up by the press more than just about anything else. I think that worked really well, and I think we got much better feedback. (Linda, Bridgeport 1)

This subtle change moved Bridgeport 1 from providing a venue for other organizations to speak, but on their topic and in their format, to allowing groups to express themselves as they wished in the format and on the topic the ally groups deemed most important. These coalition tactics helped support the local groups and their actions. And they also fostered an intense level of engagement and activism within Bridgeport 1 itself.

While Bridgeport 2 also engaged in some coalition work, it was not as central to its organization. It did not have an explicit tactic of working with other local groups, did not assign leaders within the team to the task of creating relationships with local allies, and did not work as extensively to funnel resources to other groups. Bridgeport 2 did survive until the end of the second year of mobilization; however, it was never able to create the high levels of mobilization seen in Bridgeport 1. The extent and form of coalition work within these two groups help to explain these different outcomes.

The Role of Coalitions

Using coalitions is a powerful tactic for SMOs (Hathaway and Meyer, 1993; McCammon and Campbell, 2002; Murphy, 2005; Staggenborg, 1986; Van Dyke, 2003), and the development of coalitions has long been recognized as a critical way that groups can mount large campaigns and survive over time (McAdam, 1983; Meyer, 2004; Staggenborg, 1986). Engagement in coalitions was very common among the groups in the larger Resistance, in which the Indivisible groups in this study are situated (Fisher, 2019). Coalition tactics were particularly useful given the multi-issue nature of both the original Women's March and the overall wave of contention. However, I argue that the ways in which coalitions were used differed greatly across groups and contexts.

Coalitions are not a dichotomous variable, either used or not. Groups enact this tactic to different degrees and in a variety of forms. The extent of cooperation between SMOs can vary along many dimensions (Tarrow, 2004). In particular, I focus on the breadth and depth of cooperation between groups. A coalition's breadth can be achieved by working with more distinct groups or with diverse types of actors. An Indivisible group that consistently cooperates with the American Civil Liberties Union (ACLU) on joint protest events is engaging in a relatively narrow coalition. It is regularly working with the same group with which it shares an ideology and classical SMO routes. Compare this to another Indivisible group that cooperates with ten different organizations, ranging from classic SMOs like the National Association for the Advancement of Colored People (NAACP) to businesses and civil society organizations. This second group is engaging in much broader coalition work. Past research shows that this broader coalition engagement helps a group to establish itself within community networks and can be critical for group survival (Edwards and Marullo, 1995).

Coalitions also differ in the depth of cooperation. At the lowest level of cooperation, some groups simply list the activities or events of other groups on their Facebook pages. They are not actually coordinating with these groups, but there is some support implied by listing another group's event on their pages and encouraging their members to attend. The next level of cooperation is working with a set of groups on a single joint activity such as a cosponsored town hall or speaking event. This requires cooperation and consultation between groups but is quite focused. Beyond this, some groups have long-term networks of coalition partners with whom they work on campaigns, such as voter registration drives or canvassing, that require cooperation and consultation over longer periods of time. While most work has focused on the importance of deep coalition work, some recent work highlights the benefits of more intentionally "shallow" cooperation. For example, Pullum's research (2017) on campaigns in Idaho to defeat a series of propositions found that groups intentionally limited the scope of their cooperation to facilitate the engagement of a diversity of groups and lessened the cost of working together.

Persistence is another critical dimension of variation across coalitions (Wang, Piazza, and Soule, 2018). Persistence can be related to the depth of a coalition, as deeper coalitions tend to be the result of longer-term cooperation. At one extreme, there are event coalitions, which are typically "short-lived, created for a particular protest or lobbying event" (Levi and Murphy, 2006, p. 655). At the other extreme are enduring coalitions, which involve "long-term cooperation with chosen partners" (p. 655). Event coalitions tend to be spontaneous and informal whereas enduring coalitions are typically premediated and formalized through some sort of agreement to pool resources, although this is not always the case (Levi and Murphy, 2006).

Despite the large body of work emphasizing the effectiveness of coalition tactics, some work highlights the challenges that come from working in coalitions. Reger and Staggenborg (2006), for example, found that working in coalition was successful for some National Organization of Women chapters in the short term, such as in campaigns to counter Operation Rescue in Cleveland in 1988 or in the Indiana campaign to support the Equal Rights Amendment in the 1970s. However, coalition use can also have negative long-term consequences. The groups that spent more energy creating ties with other groups were less likely to foster the internal chapter structures that worked to sustain them over time. As a result, the chapters that spent more time focusing externally on coalition development declined. Reger and Staggenborg's work highlights the ways in which the use of coalitions as a tactic is complex and situational. The present study takes this insight seriously by focusing both on how coalitions form across contexts and on their implications for group mobilization and survival.

Coalitions in Context

The local context can have important implications for the amount and type of coalition work in which a group engages. However, there is not much research that has focused on the role of context in shaping coalitions or their success. Research on coalitions more generally has shown that coalition development over time is more likely to occur in settings with histories of activism because past waves of protest can foster the development and transmission of activist knowledge and the ideologies and beliefs that support activism (Meyer, 2006). In addition, coalitions tend to form in the presence of persisting social ties (Van Dyke and Amos, 2017; Van Dyke and McCammon, 2010) and are supported by the trust that often comes from past cooperation (Levi and Murphy, 2006; Meyer and Corrigall-Brown, 2005).

Preexisting social ties can come from connections among leaders, staff, or members. Staggenborg's research (2015) on groups that mobilized around the G20 found that preexisting social ties between organizations facilitated the creation of diverse local coalitions. The dense social ties in these contexts tend to include individuals who inhabit brokerage roles between SMOs (Beamish and Luebbers, 2009; Rose, 2000; Staggenborg, 1986) or shared personnel who can transmit knowledge and skills between groups (Meyer and Boutcher, 2007; Meyer and Whittier, 1994; Whittier, 2004). Some research has referred to people who play these roles as "bridge builders," individuals who are at the nexus between two movements or organizations and are able to communicate across movement divides (Robnett, 1981; Rose, 2000; Senier et al., 2007).

Shared members can also facilitate spillover, which can help to transmit ideas, identities, tactics, or modes or organizations from group to group and facilitate cooperation. This spillover is most apparent among SMOs. However, in situations where groups do not have these types of allies available, because of either their own limited networks or the landscape of groups in their area, organizations can also benefit from spillover from less political organizations, such as charities or other civil society groups.

Coalitions within Indivisible

Many of the Indivisible groups in this study engaged actively in coalitions. However, coalition use was much more common among groups in cities with longer histories of activism. As shown in table 3.1, while 55 percent of events in these cities involved coalitions, only 35 percent of events in cities with less historical social movement mobilization used coalition tactics. In addition to the difference in the extent of coalition use, there were also vast differences in the form that coalitions took in these different contexts. In contexts with longer histories of activism, groups that work in coalition form what I refer to as "supercoalitions"— coalitions that draw upon existing networks of activists and repertoires

TABLE 3.1. Groups Founded, Survival, and Coalition Use, by City

	Extensive History of Activism	Little History of Activism	All Cities
Groups Founded	23	12	35
Coalition Use in City	55%	35%	48%

of action and work to funnel resources and expertise from newly mobilized to existing groups. Cities where these supercoalitions emerge tend to have more events and are more likely to have their groups survive over time.

Groups in areas without these histories of activism engage in less coalition work on average and, as a result, have fewer events and less group survival over time. However, this content is not determinative. Groups in these areas can use coalitions to counter some of these trends. In these areas, groups that use coalitions engage in broader coalition work where they partner with civil society allies and work to normalize activism. When groups do this within contexts with little history of activism, they are able to mount more events and have higher levels of group survival over time. Figure 3.1 outlines the model presented in this chapter. These findings support my overall argument that coalitions are elements of city contexts, not just group tactics. And the ways in which groups engage in coalitions is context dependent.

How City Context Shapes Coalitions

I begin by examining the ways in which cities with a long history of activism were able to harness existing ties and networks to facilitate the creation of deep and sustained coalitions. This occurred in Pasadena, Pittsburgh, Atlanta, and Bridgeport. The coalitions in these cities emerged through a managed effort of working with already-existing groups and adopting a tactic of trying to support diverse allies and voices. The outcome of these tactics was a very particular kind of

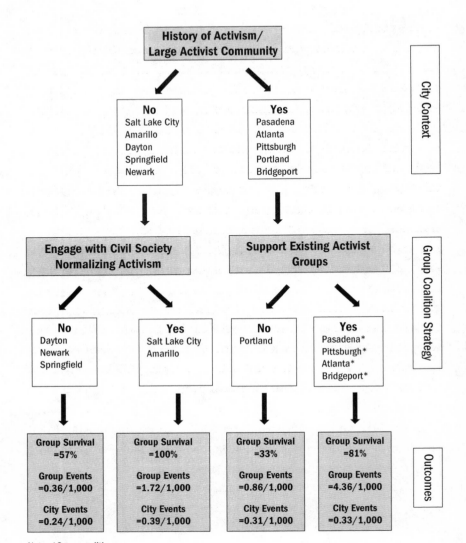

Note: *Supercoalitions

FIGURE 3.1. Model of Coalition Strategies and Outcomes, by City

coalition, the supercoalition. In part because of this tactic, the groups in these cities were much more likely to survive over time (with 81 percent of groups making it to the second anniversary of the march) and tended to have a high number of events (0.33 events/1,000 population). I also examine the outlier, Portland, Oregon, where there are deep activist roots, but where activists were unable to create, or uninterested in creating, coalitions. Instead, internal divisions limited cooperation and, as a result, the groups in Portland were much less likely to survive over time (with only 29 percent making it to the second anniversary of the march). However, there were still many large events in the city (0.31 events/1,000 population).

I then turn to examining the cities without histories of activism and how groups in these cities fared in the two years after the first Women's March. In general, groups in these cities were less likely to engage in widespread coalition work. This was the case in Dayton, Newark, and Springfield. In these cities, none of the groups engaged in high levels of coalition activity. Moreover, groups in these cities were not very likely to survive (only 57 percent made it to the second anniversary of the march) and did not tend to have many events (0.24 events/1,000 population).

The lack of activist history in the city was not always detrimental to group mobilization. In Salt Lake City and, to some extent, in Amarillo, activists did engage in a particular kind of broad coalition work. This broad coalition tactic focused on partnering with a large diversity of civil society actors. Some of these actors were political, but most of them were apolitical, such as libraries, charities, businesses, and religious groups. The outcome of broad and often nonpolitical coalition work was that the groups normalized activism in a context in which there were fewer past activists and events with which people were familiar. In part because of this tactic, the groups in these cities were much more likely to survive over time (with 100 percent of groups making it to the second anniversary march) and tended to have high numbers of events (0.39 events/1,000 population). In fact, the groups in the cities without a history of activism that engaged in this broad coalition work had higher

TABLE 3.2. QCA Pathways for Group Survival and Group Events

OUTCOME = Group Survival	Coverage	Consistency	Exemplar Cities	Outlier Cities
SUPPORTACTGROUPS*civilsociety	0.70	1	Pittsburgh, Atlanta, Bridgeport, Pasadena	
historyofactivism*supportactgrps*CIVILSOCIETY	0.22	1	SLC, Amarillo	
Solution	0.91	1		

OUTCOME = Number of Events	Coverage	Consistency	Exemplar Cities	Outlier Cities
HISTORYOFACTIVISM*civilsociety	0.85	0.85	Pittsburgh, Atlanta, Bridgeport	Pasadena, SLC
Solution	0.85	0.85		

Uppercase letters indicate the presence of a condition and lowercase letters indicate its absence. An asterisk (*) indicates "and." The table also presents consistency and coverage, two key concepts in the QCA. Consistency is the percentage of the causal configurations with the specific composition that results in the same outcome variable. Coverage is the number of cases for which the configuration is valid (Roig-Tierno, Gonzalez-Cruz, and Llopis-Martinez, 2017).

survival rates and more events per 1,000 people than any other group of cities—even those cities with long histories of activism.

These findings are supported by the Qualitative Comparative Analysis (QCA) examining the multiple pathways to groups' survival and number of events. The QCA, presented in table 3.2, illustrates the two main pathways to group survival.[1] First, groups could work extensively with already-existing activist groups and avoid cooperation with nonpolitical civil society partners. This was the pathway of 70 percent of the groups that survived and was the tactic of groups in Pasadena, Pittsburgh, Atlanta, and Bridgeport. The second route to survival occurred among groups in areas without much history of activism. In these areas, groups that did not work with existing activist groups but did engage with nonpolitical civil society organizations were also able to survive. This route accounts for 22 percent of the surviving groups. This was a tactic employed by groups in Salt Lake City and Amarillo. Together, these two pathways have 100 percent consistency and account for 92 percent of the groups. The QCA highlights that the tactic of working with existing activist groups or with civil society organizations is differentially successful, depending on the context in which the activism takes place.

The QCA examining the routes to achieving a high number of events in a city shows that there is one main route to extensive mobilization. Groups in cities with long histories of activism that do not partner with nonpolitical civil society actors were able to mobilize large numbers of events. This route accounts for 85 percent of the groups and has 85 percent consistency. It does not account for the surprisingly low number of events in Pasadena or the surprisingly high number of events in Salt Lake City. Let's turn to a more in-depth consideration of each city to better understand the dynamics at play in these different contexts.

Histories of Activism, Supporting Existing Groups, and the Supercoalition

The city context shapes the options available to groups if they decide to embark upon creating coalitions. In areas where there is a long history of activism, groups have many possible partners from which to choose.[2] And they may even have past relationships upon which to draw when creating coalitions. This was certainly the case in Pasadena, Pittsburgh, Atlanta, and Bridgeport.

The history of activist work, and the wealth of experience that many activists in these areas have, also brought an understanding of the modern norms of leftist activism. These activists often discussed how they sought to partner with local groups who were different from them along racial, ethnic, immigrant, sexual orientation, class, or other dimensions. These activists recognized the lack of diversity within the membership of some of the groups and were conscious of not wanting to usurp other groups who were already mobilized and, potentially, more in touch with certain sets of issues, such as BLM, Deferred Action for Childhood Arrivals (DACA), or the LGBTQ+ community. This led these groups to partner with existing political organizations already working in their communities and to embrace a strategy of division of labor in which they brought financial and human resources to support the work of long-standing community organizations, many of which were much more diverse than they were.

The result of this work was the creation of supercoalitions. These supercoalitions did not tend to directly mobilize people to the streets (or town halls or congressional offices). Instead they focused on mobilizing resources, bringing groups together, and lending support to other organizations. This focus on organization building and resource allocation, in part, accounts for the very high level of group survival in these areas and the high number of events. The following section examines these dynamics in Pittsburgh and Pasadena.[3]

Pittsburgh

Pittsburgh has a long history as a vibrant community for activism. This helped facilitate the mobilization of the city's five Indivisible groups by providing many available partners for cooperation, long-standing ties between groups, and a wealth of activist experience. The groups in Pittsburgh engaged in considerable coalition work; an average of 55 percent of the events in Pittsburgh involved working with coalition partners.[4] Pittsburgh had three large supercoalition groups (two Indivisible groups from this study and another supercoalition group that did not start as an Indivisible group). These supercoalitions engaged actively with existing political groups in their community but did not often cooperate with mainstream civil society organizations (such as charities or religious institutions). While these supercoalition groups did not tend to have many events themselves, they worked to funnel resources to other groups and highlight their work. As a result, the city as a whole had a very high number of events (0.40 per 1,000 population), the second highest number of events per 1,000 people of any city in this study. While some Indivisible groups in this city did work alone (such as Pittsburgh 5, which only worked in a coalition for 19 percent of their events and had 135 events), extensive cooperation was a general feature of the groups in this city.

The creation of supercoalitions in Pittsburgh started with the recognition among some of the early founders that the Indivisible groups tied to the first Women's March offered both exciting possibilities but also challenges. On the one hand, these groups were harnessing the enthusiasm and energy of a large and powerful group of people. On the other hand, those who mobilized tended to be more homogeneous than desirable, given the diversity of issues at hand and the different constituents that they hoped to reach. As a result, the early founders in Pittsburgh began trying to expand their networks and reach out to already-mobilized groups within the city. They did this in a number of ways.

First, some original founding members joined other preexisting activist groups in the city. As Debbie, who was actively involved in one of the Pittsburgh supercoalition groups, explains, "What I saw was predominantly women who already were working for a living and fully engaged, desperately trying to reach other likeminded women, not knowing the rules and algorithms of Facebook, not being on Twitter and never having done this before. They were popping up like popcorn. I was watching them online and joining every single one. By the end of January, I had joined about twenty groups." These groups ranged from other local Indivisible organizations to groups focused on women's issues, LGBTQ+ causes, labor rights, and BLM. This tactic had powerful results. Within three months, Debbie estimates that "we could get our message out not only to our followers but on to the pages of 19,000 others. It was proving quite powerful." While Debbie did not engage in collective actions with these other groups, being a member on their Facebook pages allowed her to have access to a much larger group of potential activists when she was publicizing events and working to foster cooperation across groups.

Second, the Pittsburgh groups attempted to plug into other networks of activists through existing organizations. Michelle, who was active in a supercoalition in Pittsburgh, explains how she attended a local County Democrats event. At this event, she and others from her organization went around the room inviting groups to join the Indivisible cause. Kim's group used a similar tactic to expand the networks of allies: "We partnered with Planned Parenthood, we partnered with immigrant advocacy organizations, with antipoverty groups, and we also showed up for things that were going on elsewhere in the district, labor-related things." This tactic was also used at protest events such as the March for Science or the March for Our Lives. Activists from the Pittsburgh Indivisible groups collected names and contact information from other organizations at these large protest events for later cooperation.

The concentrated effort to partner with many diverse groups was common across the Indivisible groups in Pittsburgh, particularly the two Indivisible groups that became supercoalitions (and the additional group in the city that was a supercoalition but did not start as an Indivisible group). This was the result of explicit efforts to expand cooperation. Once a smaller set of groups was mobilized, meetings would end with a call to add more members and to brainstorm where new groups and members could be found.

The creation of coalitions was facilitated by a division of labor within each organization and the movement in Pittsburgh as a whole. Within groups, there was a conscious decision to prioritize the creation of coalition ties by assigning a person within the Indivisible group the task of making strategic connections with other groups. The importance of creating a division of labor among organizational leadership has long been understood as critical for groups to effectively mobilize and survive over time (see, for example, Gose and Skocpol, 2019; Reger and Staggenborg, 2006) and this tactic was at work in the Indivisible groups in Pittsburgh. For example, Michelle, in a large Pittsburgh supercoalition, was put in charge of "recruiting and strategic partnerships."

At the more macro level, the development of supercoalitions was based on the idea that it was strategic to have a division of labor at the city and state levels. For example, the Pittsburgh groups came together to create the "Neighborhood Club," a local supercoalition that did not organize any events but brought together groups to coordinate activities, share resources, and strategize. This Neighborhood Club was created through an open invitation on Facebook. It was intentionally given a very benign and nondescript name so as to avoid attracting trolls online. Then, as Michelle explains, "when everyone was in the room, we got contact information." While the initial meeting brought together an impressive thirty groups, they immediately began brainstorming new groups to recruit and continued to expand.

The power of the supercoalition is in its ability to mobilize resources to other groups and coordinate strategies. As Donna describes, supercoalitions were an important online presence that could connect people to other groups or events. They worked to coordinate with smaller groups or groups with fewer resources and to help mobilize members and resources to their events. They also engaged in activities like postcard campaigns that "promoted what other folks are doing to help get turnout all throughout the area. Some people cared more about the environment; some people wanted to do more on social justice. But when we have actions, we reach out to all these groups and then we promote door knocking and canvassing for all of the Democratic events that are going on" (Donna, Pittsburgh 4).

What was interesting about the supercoalitions in this city is that they did not host many events themselves. However, I argue that their presence in the city led to high overall rates of mobilization. Pittsburgh had the second highest number of events per 1,000 population (0.40/1,000), as recorded by Count Love, a database of protest events in the United States by city (https://countlove.org/). I argue that this can be attributed to the particular tactic of supercoalitions that worked to harness existing relationships with political groups, build new ties within the activist community, and channel resources to groups that were already mobilizing.

Pasadena

Pasadena is a city with a long and vibrant history of civic engagement. After the first Women's March, three Indivisible groups were founded in the city. Two of these groups engaged actively in coalitions (88 percent and 94 percent of their activities, respectively) and had many events (180 and 583 events). The final group, Pasadena 2, did not engage in any coalition activities. This group hosted very few events (twelve) and did not survive until the second anniversary march. Pasadena had a supercoalition, like the one in Pittsburgh, and used similar tactics for reaching out to existing active political groups. However, the underlying ideology of recognizing privilege and waging that privilege to highlight the work of other groups was more central to the work of the Pasadena groups than it was among the groups in Pittsburgh. Additionally, their tactic of channeling resources to other preexisting groups was also more explicit in the general functioning of their group.

Just like the groups in Pittsburgh, the Indivisible groups in Pasadena intentionally worked to create ties with existing activist organizations in the community. As Steve, from Pasadena 1, explains,

> I'm very active with police reform. And then just from going to meetings on that you meet this person who is at the ACLU, this person at Planned Parenthood, this person at an immigration reform group. It's the whole networking thing. Just getting into other spaces. We have a person in our group who is very active with Swing Left, she comes in and brings in twenty other groups and the environmental guy brings in fifteen other groups. So it balloons very quickly.

In Pasadena, the organizers were even more explicit about the ideological reasons for trying to expand networks. There was a conscious effort not to duplicate the work or to supplant other groups. Steve explains that Pasadena 1 knew that

> we're not going to be the leaders on most of these issues and, honestly, we shouldn't be the leaders on immigration or racial justice issues. Those groups should be led by the people who have the most skin in the game. We're a predominantly white group, being Pasadena. So we shouldn't be

leading Black Lives Matter marches, we shouldn't be going and telling everyone what to say at an immigration thing. The group that we have, we all kind of agreed, we need to know our place and kind of support.

The group subscribed to a policy of "cooperate, don't co-op. Support, don't supplant." Melodie reinforces this mantra when she notes that many of the "go-to organizations seemed to be run by older white people, and we wanted to have a diverse base of people engaged and feel connected to the activist community. That was a very intentional choice on our part to invite a lot more of those groups who are doing work with younger populations that maybe have been overlooked in the activist network in Pasadena in the past."

This tactic of partnering with existing groups was based on ideology, but it was also practical. These preexisting groups already knew the issues, the actors, and the history in Pasadena. As Steve explains, "It's much easier just pragmatically to just reach out to them and say, 'Hey, what's going on in this and do you need support?' And it was kind of the whole idea of we're all in this together and there's a lot of overlap."

The cooperation with existing local groups and working to bring resources and attention to those groups led to the desire to found a supercoalition. This began when the local Pasadena activists joined with others in adjacent areas to create cooperation across communities. It took over a year to form this coalition, but it now meets four times a year and works to share resources, connect groups, and encourage larger strategic thinking. The supercoalition originated at a conference of progressive groups in another California city in 2018. The leaders began by bringing together representatives from twelve local groups whom they had met at this conference. They immediately encouraged this initial group to use their networks to attract a larger collection of local community organizations. Now, any groups that are willing to sign a broad "values pledge" agreeing to a set of progressive values are welcome to join. It has been very successful, with fifty groups participating in the 2019 quarterly meetings.

The meetings for the Pasadena supercoalition focus on resource sharing. As Melodie explains, the supercoalition "is a way for us to all share resources and support each other and make sure we're coordinating, so we're not stepping on each other's toes. If someone is doing an action, then they would have half the people that we could get if we did one together." The meetings begin with a meet and greet where groups can introduce themselves and their cause. Then there is a resource swap where all groups can list resources that they need or have. Other groups walk around the room and see what is needed (perhaps a microphone for an event or 1,000 people for a protest) and sign up to help where they can.

The group also hosts a resource database online. All groups list the resources they have to share with their coalition allies. Melodie, who also works for Planned Parenthood in the area, understood the significance of resource sharing early. As part of a large and well-established group, she recognizes that her organization has access to resources such as sound equipment and venues in addition to vast experience organizing events. She began by offering other groups access to these resources but soon recognized that this sharing could happen on a much larger scale through an online tool. As Melodie explains,

> The organizations basically put in everything from "I have a venue," "I have an inflatable, blow-up projection screen for movie viewings outside," or "I have tables and chairs" to "I have volunteers who are ready to take action" or "I have a speaker who would be great." We got very abstract in what we define as a resource because if you're doing any of these things, there may be a million different physical or abstract things that we need to be able to accomplish something. Any of our members can log in and look and see, does anyone have that thing that I need? Then reach out and ask if it's available.

There is also an online membership calendar where all groups can list their events and call for other groups to join with them in their actions. The quarterly supercoalition meetings end with shared training, such as methods for retaining members, how to use social media to mobilize, or engaging in research on policy issues. This provides value for groups to attend and participate, even if they do not need resources or have resources to share.

In order to deal with the many challenges that may come from co-operation across groups, the Pasadena supercoalition began with some ground rules. First, only one representative from each group needs to attend the meetings. This reduces the burden on each participating group. Second, the member groups agree that they will communicate directly only with the organizational leaders and not with individual members. This alleviates the concern that many groups had about "volunteer poaching." Finally, the supercoalition agrees not to endorse any specific action or event. There is a recognition that, while all the groups agree to the general values pledge and progressive ideals, there is still a wide diversity of views within the group. By agreeing not to specifically endorse any action in particular, the supercoalition remains an open and inclusive space for all groups. As Melodie explains, "We recognize that each group is bringing something to the table that is a bit different, but we're not there to decide what's the best way forward. We're just there to decide how do we continue to support the good work that everyone's doing in a smarter and more cooperative way."

This supercoalition format and general cooperation was very effective in Pasadena. There was high survival in the city as a whole (two out of three groups survived) and a high number of events hosted by these groups (5.6 per 1,000). It is interesting that, while there was high mobilization among these groups, there was a small number of events in the city as a whole, as measured by Count Love (0.15 events/1,000 population). Count Love is much more likely to include larger events as it uses media coverage to identify events. The Pasadena groups had many more organizational meetings and smaller events, which created a vibrant local context even without large protests. In addition, Pasadena's proximity to Los Angeles could account for why there was a lot of grass-roots mobilization but fewer events, as activists regularly went to LA for larger protests and marches.

Histories of Activism and Working Alone

Portland

Portland is clearly a city with a long and active history of mobilization and protest. Because of this, it is not surprising that Portland founded the most Indivisible groups of any city in this study after the first Women's March, with seven groups founded in the city. However, what is interesting about the groups in Portland is that they very rarely worked in coalition with one another or with other groups in the city. In fact, four of the seven Indivisible groups *never* worked with coalition partners. These four groups were all formed around a feminist collective identity and focused on creating a safe space for women to connect and support one another instead of on outward political action. As Portland Indivisible 2 explains on its Facebook page, it provides "a space for women to discuss politics and current events—opportunities to use our influence to make a better world." Its events are "weekly meet-ups to discuss politics, volunteerism and activism—as well as personal experiences. This is a space for women to support and motivate each other and celebrate our influence in the world."

Of the other three Indivisible groups in the city, two worked occasionally with partners (10 percent and 14 percent of their activities, respectively), and only one group worked consistently with coalition partners (66 percent of their events in the first two years). The two groups with the most cooperation survived and thrived, hosting 264 and 235 events in the first two years. This illustrates how coalition work can be critical for group mobilization. The Facebook page for the most coalition-focused group, Portland 6, describes its "Coalition for Immigrants Rights: Popular Assembly" as addressing immigration needs and plans for specific types of action, such as legislation. The goal of the event was not to duplicate efforts but to band together to be as efficient as possible. At this event and others, Portland 6 emphasizes collaboration with other organizations like Indivisible Oregon, Oregon Peace Institution, and Students United for Nonviolence.

Portland 7 rarely worked in coalitions, engaging in this tactic for only 14 percent of its events, but was still sensitive to the need to amalgamate resources and empower other groups. This group survived until the end of the second year and was also able to host many events (264 events in the two years). For example, in the event "Indigenous Women's March: Honoring Red Fawn and Indigenous Women Warriors" the group worked to empower local Indigenous activists. It explains on its Facebook page that "Portland's Woman's March has NOT been cancelled, it has stepped aside to support in solidarity to create space for Indigenous women to be seen and heard. Come march with us in solidarity for the women's warriors who were before us and who are still paving the path for us to march forward." This illustrates how the group was attempting to create space for collaboration with other social movement allies. Overall, Portland 7 engaged in the same types of techniques of resource sharing as the other groups in cities with long histories of activism; however, it did not do this as consistently or use it as a core tactic.

Despite the coalition activities of a few of the groups in Portland, the city as a whole was not characterized by high levels of cooperation. I argue that the lack of cooperation across the city is one reason why groups in Portland did not tend to survive over time. Only two of the seven Indivisible groups in Portland survived until the second anniversary event. However, it is important to note that Portland did still have a relatively high number of events (0.31 events/1,000 population). Portland demonstrates how cities with very long histories of activism and large activist communities can still mount large events without engaging in extensive coalition work. These areas are just less likely to have groups survive over time.

No Histories of Activism and Working Alone

In cities without extensive histories of activism, groups were generally less likely to engage in widespread coalition work. This was the case in Dayton, Newark, and Springfield. In these cities, none of the groups engaged in high levels of cooperation with other groups. Moreover in these contexts, groups were not as likely to survive (only 57 percent made it to the second anniversary march), and there were not many events in the cities as a whole (0.16 events/1,000 population).

However, the lack of an activist history in the city is not determinative. In Salt Lake City and, to some extent, Amarillo, activists did engage in a particular kind of broad coalition work. These broad coalitions focused on partnering with a large diversity of civil society actors. Some of these actors were political, but most of them were apolitical, such as libraries, charities, businesses, and religious groups. The outcome of this tactic of broad, and often nonpolitical, coalition work was that the groups normalized activism in a context in which there were fewer past activists upon which to draw and events with which locals were familiar. In part because of this tactic, the groups in these cities were very likely to survive over time (with 100 percent of groups making it to the second anniversary of the march) and tended to have high numbers of events at the city level (0.28 events/1,000 population). In fact, the groups in the cities without a history of activism that engaged in this broad coalition work had higher survival and more events per 1,000 people than any other group of cities—even those cities with a long history of activism. In order to understand this, I begin by examining the modal pathway in cities without activist histories, where there was very little coalition work. I then turn to the alternative pathway, which occurred in Salt Lake City and Amarillo, where groups employed the broad coalition tactic with very successful results.

Dayton

In Dayton, three Indivisible groups were founded after the first Women's March. None of these groups engaged in *any* coalition work and they had very few events (ten, ten, and four events, respectively). These groups were each focused on a single issue. For example, Dayton 1 was a longtime reproductive rights organization that became an Indivisible

group after the first Women's March. However, it never hosted or participated in events on other topics beyond reproductive rights. Moreover,
while it did mention the work of the local Planned Parenthood chapter
on their Facebook page on two occasions, it never cooperated with the
group on actions. The Dayton groups were also notable in their very low
level of discussion on their Facebook pages, with most events having no
description or comments. Dayton, as a city, had 0.33 events per 1,000
population, which is in the middle to low range, and none of its groups
survived until the second anniversary march.

Newark

Newark had two Indivisible groups, which is quite low, given the large
population of the city. For a comparison, similarly sized Pittsburgh
(populations of 302,000 vs. 285,000) had five Indivisible groups. The
groups in Newark also engaged in very little coalition work. Newark 1
only worked in coalition for 7 percent of their activities, hosted five
events, and did not survive until the second anniversary. Newark 2 did
even less coalition work, cooperating on only one action in the two years
under study. This group did manage to host a larger number of events
(102) and survive until the second anniversary march. Despite the low
level of protest in Newark, there is a very supportive political landscape
for these types of progressive movements. For example, Newark mayor
Ras Baraka was a vocal opponent of Trump and called out Trump's
response to the violent protests in Charlottesville. Yet Newark was not
able to mount a large-scale sustained mobilization over the two years of
the study.

Springfield

Springfield had two Indivisible groups. Neither engaged in much coalition work (35 percent and 0 percent, respectively), and the groups hosted
relatively few events over the two years (seventeen and thirty-five,

respectively). They were also single-issue groups, with both focusing almost exclusively on health care. It is notable that, despite the fact that these groups were both focused on the same core issue, there was no cooperation between them in the two years under analysis. These groups did, however, survive until the second anniversary.

No Histories of Activism and Supporting Civil Society

While there were some outliers, the general trend is that in cities with little history of activism, there tended to be very little coalition work. And these cities usually had low numbers of events and low survival rates. However, the lack of an activist history in the city could be navigated through intentional strategies by activists. In Salt Lake City and, to some extent, in Amarillo, activists engaged in broad coalition work with very successful results.

Salt Lake City, which has very little activist history, had exceptionally high levels of mobilization. In fact, the rate of 0.71 events per 1,000 population was over two times as high as any other city in the sample, including Atlanta, Pittsburgh, and Portland, where there are long histories of activist mobilizations. What explains this surprisingly high rate of mobilization and group survival? One of the key factors was the use of coalitions in Salt Lake City. However, because of the local context, activists in Salt Lake employed very different coalition strategies from those used in Pittsburgh, Pasadena, Atlanta, and Bridgeport. Instead of the deep "supercoalition" tactic used in these other cities, they engaged in a broad coalitional form that saw them actively cooperate with nonpolitical civil society actors in an attempt to normalize activism and appeal to previously nonengaged members of the public. This tactic was also employed by some, but not all, of the groups in Amarillo. I argue that this is why Amarillo experienced only some of the benefits of coalition work, with high group survival but fewer events (only 0.06 events/1,000 population). I begin by examining these two cities to explore how cities without histories of activism can still use coalitions strategically and effectively.

Salt Lake City

In Salt Lake City, there were very high levels of coalition work among all three Indivisible groups. Each of the groups engaged in coalition work in almost all of their activities (97 percent, 88 percent, and 86 percent, respectively). They all also hosted very high numbers of events (270, 170, and 182, respectively). The city as a whole was exceptionally active, the most active of any city in this study, despite a less conducive context for engagement. I argue that this was the result of an explicitly broad coalition form that worked to normalize activism and make engagement seem less political.

The three groups in Salt Lake City were effective at bridging the political/nonpolitical divide. They did this by engaging with both political institutions and groups inside and outside traditional politics. They also cooperated with apolitical civil society institutions, such as libraries, universities, and charities. In these ways, the groups in Salt Lake were integrated with other groups and organizations in the city and were able to bridge the divide that sometimes exists between the political and nonpolitical. As Andrew, in Salt Lake City 2, explains, this helped to "normalize activism. I think the leadership is smart for that reason because they realize that, you know, the more it becomes partisan, the more you are just fighting, not bringing people together in a common cause."

Specifically, Indivisible groups in Salt Lake City partnered with a wide range of civil society actors. Salt Lake City 1, for example, cohosted events with the Democratic Party, supported candidates for office, and ran town halls with elected officials. However, they also engaged with social movement groups such as the Sierra Club, the ACLU, and Planned Parenthood. What is most interesting about the Salt Lake groups is their willingness to cooperate with nonpolitical groups. For instance, they engaged extensively with the Salt Lake City library. The library cohosted a number of nonpolitical events, such as an event about a new law lowering the legal blood alcohol content level to 0.05 with Salt Lake City 1 and a women's history month event moderated by a local radio host with Salt Lake City 2. Both events were focused on nonpolitical topics but included political actors (such as elected officials and activists). Salt Lake City 2 also hosted a totally nonpolitical educational event about wolf packs at a Salt Lake City public library (November 2). These types of events brought out local residents so they could come in contact with the Indivisible group members and their ideas in a nonpolitical context.

The Salt Lake City groups also hosted events that bridged the political and nonpolitical divide. For example, a local neighborhood house hosted a series of talks listed on Salt Lake City 1's Facebook page (March 30). The talks discussed creating a Neighborhood Watch association to reduce crime; starting a consulting business; making health and body products, chocolate, and beer; and lobbying for social change. The final event taught individuals how to engage in political lobbying, presented right after a beer-tasting event. Come for the beer, stay for the activism!

The Salt Lake City groups also cooperated with businesses, which might be seen as an unusual ally for organizations on the political left. Salt Lake City 1 cooperated with Patagonia (March 7) and coordinated with business groups such as Womenpreneurs (April 4) and the Salt Lake Chamber Business Women's Forum (March 21). Salt Lake City 1 also hosted an event on January 31 that was sponsored by Zions Bank—an "emerging leader's initiative" aimed to get young professionals engaged in their community.

By engaging various segments of civil society, many of which were not political, the Salt Lake City Indivisible groups broadened access to political engagement and destigmatized activism for people who might otherwise have been wary of progressive causes, given the state's conservative context. In fact, Salt Lake City 2 and 3 were some of the only groups in this study that were expressly nonpartisan. Two of the three groups in Salt Lake City felt that "they would lose credibility to be tied to the Democratic party in a very red area. We would say no to a listing if it was blatantly partisan, especially on the Democratic side" (Andrew, Salt Lake City 2). This enabled these two Indivisible groups to create coalitions with organizations that normally worked with Republican officials and causes. For example, Salt Lake City 3 worked with Mormon Women for Ethical Government. This group usually works only with Republican officials. However, as Stefanie explains, "They were outraged at Trump's behavior and saw fighting him as a nonpartisan cause." The group also had Republican members, something that did not occur among groups in any of the other cities in the sample. That gave the group access to Republican elected officials because group members were not seen as "crazy liberals" (Stefanie, Salt Lake City 3). This broad and often nonpolitical coalition tactic was very effective and led to high group survival as well as very high numbers of events within these groups and within the city as a whole.

Amarillo

Amarillo is another city that does not have a long and active history of mobilization. There were two Indivisible groups founded in Amarillo after the first Women's March. Both groups engaged in coalition partnerships in about half of their events (49 percent and 56 percent, respectively). However, the number of events hosted differed greatly across the two groups. While Amarillo 1 hosted fifty-six events in the first two years, Amarillo 2 only hosted nine. Both groups survived until the second anniversary march. However, this is a very different level of mobilization. While Amarillo 1 engaged actively with civil society organizations and saw itself as nonpartisan, Amarillo 2 mobilized only explicitly political and partisan events. Amarillo highlights how it is not simply using coalitions that leads to successful outcomes. Instead, it is *how* a group engages in coalitions, and who it partners with, that can lead to effective mobilization over time.

Amarillo 1 worked in coalition for about half of its events. These coalitions were very broad. As Peter explains, "A couple of our members are involved with other organizations, like the League of Women's Voters, the NAACP, we kind of share the same vision, the same mantra. So it's good to have those other groups. And they bring different ideas, different resources, different individuals." Barbara (Amarillo 1) describes how people from different groups come together as part of a steering committee in their group: "We all work together. If you're working, if you're operating in a vacuum, you're not getting very far."

There is a clear focus on coalition work in Amarillo 1, and this work was sometimes political and partisan. However, there was a concern in the group that engaging in activism that is seen as too radical could be deleterious. The fear is that this would "turn off" members of the community who tend to be more conservative. As Peter explains, they would "lose credibility if they were seen to be too extreme" by working on issues such as impeachment. However, the group was still partisan and hosted partisan events such as rallies for Beto O'Rourke (which it did seven times in the period leading up to the state election). Despite a fear of being seen as too radical, activists in Amarillo 1 felt that they had to engage in partisan work. As Barbara explains, in the conservative context of Amarillo, "we are the only ones who will do it." However, they paired this work with less political and broader coalition activities.

Amarillo 2 engaged in only political activities and tended to be much more radical in its rhetoric. The group actively supported impeachment and its Facebook page is filled with humor about Trump and the Republican Party as a whole. Members did work in coalition with other groups, and many members were also part of Amarillo 1. However, Amarillo 2 as a group hosted only political events and had very few activities over the period of this study.

Conclusion: The Role of Coalitions

Coalitions are a powerful mobilizing tactic. However, the ways that coalitions are used and the form that they take differ greatly across contexts. The importance of local context has not been the focus of past work on coalitions and the present study illuminates how coalition strategies, and the implications of these strategies, are highly context dependent. I argue that there were two main forms that coalitions could take and that

TABLE 3.3. Group Features and Survival, by City

City	Group Number	Coalition Use	Citywide Events*	Group Events	Survival
		History of Activism + Supercoalitions			
Pittsburgh	1	93	122	14	No
	2	66		3	No
	3	96		45	Yes
	4	95		18	Yes
	5	19		135	Yes
	City Total		0.40/1000	0.711/1000	3/5
Pasadena	1	88	21	180	Yes
	2	0		12	No
	3	94		583	Yes
	City Total		0.15/1000	5.6/1000	2/3
Atlanta	1	91	190	126	Yes
	2	70		85	Yes
	3	90		267	Yes
	4	62		78	Yes
	5	86		36	Yes
	6	98		53	Yes
	City Total		0.39/1000	1.15/1000	6/6
Bridgeport	1	92	17	619	Yes
	2	35		17	Yes
	City Total		0.37/1000	4.36/1000	2/2
		History of Activism + No Supercoalitions			
Portland	1	10	199	39	No
	2	0		12	No
	3	0		1	No
	4	0		19	No
	5	0		2	No
	6	66		235	Yes
	7	14		264	Yes
	City Total		0.31/1000	0.86/1000	2/7
		No History of Activism + No Engagement with Civil Society Actors			
Dayton	1	0	46	10	No
	2	0		10	No
	3	0		4	No
	City Total		0.33/1000	0.17/1000	0/3
Newark	1	7	41	15	No
	2	1		102	Yes
	City Total		0.14/1000	0.41/1000	1/2
Springfield	1	35	40	17	Yes
	2	0		38	Yes
	City Total		0.35/1000	0.48/1000	2/2
		No History of Activism + Engagement with Civil Society Actors			
Amarillo	1	49	12	56	Yes
	2	56		9	Yes
	City Total		0.06/1000	0.32/1000	2/2
Salt Lake City	1	97	144	270	Yes
	2	88		170	Yes
	3	86		182	Yes
	City Total		0.72/1000	3.11/1000	3/3

*Based on Count Love data, https://countlove.org/.

the effectiveness of these forms was very situational. First, groups could work extensively in coalition with already-existing activist groups and avoid cooperation with nonpolitical civil society partners. This was a common tactic among the groups in cities with long and active histories of mobilization, such as Pasadena, Pittsburgh, Atlanta, and Bridgeport. The second route to survival occurred among groups in areas without much history of activism. In these areas, groups that did not work with existing political activist groups but did engage with nonpolitical civil society organizations were also able to survive. This was the coalition form used by groups in Salt Lake City and one of the groups in Amarillo. This research highlights how there are multiple routes to survival for groups over time and that working with existing activist groups or with civil society organizations is differentially successful, depending on the context in which the activism takes place.

This chapter illustrates how coalitions are very effective tactics but also how the ways that coalitions are used differ across political contexts. Interviews with activists illuminate these different ways that coalitions can be used. In cities with long histories of activism, groups tended to engage in more coalition work and a particular type of deep coalition, the supercoalition. This form of coalition focuses on strategically coordinating groups within a city, supporting existing groups, and channeling resources to other organizations. In cities without long histories of activism, groups are less likely to engage in coalition work. However, this context was not determinative. When groups did engage in coalitions in these contexts, they tended to organize into broad civil society coalitions that brought together a diversity of political and nonpolitical actors. These broad coalitions were very successful at mobilizing people and helping groups survive over time.

4

Becoming Indivisible

Facilitating Recruitment and Persistence among Members

Portland seems like a perfect place to engage in progressive activism. The city is known for its vibrant political scene and has been the site of many large and dramatic protests. One such event was the first Portland Women's March in 2017, which was an unmitigated success. It brought over 100,000 people to the streets and was the largest protest event in Portland history. As the *Portland Tribune* reported, "The rain-soaked event took on a festive atmosphere. So many people attended that it was impossible for everyone to see or hear speakers on the stage south of the Morrison Bridge. At 1:15 p.m., the official start time of the march, thousands were still crammed motionless in Waterfront Park" (Pamplin Media Group, 2017).

Activists in Portland seized the moment after this march, founding seven Indivisible chapters along with many other groups in the city aimed at challenging the policies of the new president. These activists worked to mount a series of large protest events in the city. Six hundred people protested the Muslim ban at the Portland airport in January, the Not My President's Day march filled the streets in February, and thousands appeared at the March for Science in April. The May Day protests in the city were so large that they were shut down by local police who characterized them as riots and who arrested twenty-five protesters. Various pro-Trump events were also peppered in between the progressive protests, creating a vibrant and often contentious climate in Portland in 2017 and 2018.

The organizers in Portland, both in the Indivisible groups and beyond, focused on large and dramatic events. They pursued campaigns that brought very progressive ideals to the fore and did not shy away from challenging powerful institutions of society, such as capitalism and patriarchy. They also actively resisted the mobilizations of conservative contingents in the city, counterprotesting their events and clashing with Trump supporters.

In many ways, the Portland Indivisible groups were quite successful. The events in Portland were very large. In fact, the Portland Indivisible groups mobilized an average of 500 people per event, the second highest average in the study. However, while activism in the city remained vibrant over this period, the Indivisible groups themselves did not fare as well. In fact, five of the seven Indivisible groups in the city had disbanded by the second anniversary march. There are a variety of reasons for this. First, there was some vigorous infighting in the groups, with accusations of racism and transphobia being leveled against leaders in one group and concerns over misappropriation of funds in another (Acker, 2019). In addition, the remaining groups embraced increasingly radical tactics and issues. And, while this did facilitate large and dramatic events, it did not help to expand the movement to those outside traditional progressive circles. Finally, the groups spent most of their energy on mobilizing large events and did not invest in developing organizations or facilitating the engagement of their members, leading to high rates of turnover in the groups.

The Portland case illustrates the complex decisions that social movement actors must make. Social movement organizations (SMOs) are engaged in the dual functions of mobilizing and organizing (Han, 2014). Mobilizing is the transactional focus on maximizing the number of people engaged in civic action. Organizing is the transformational focus on developing the capacities of people to engage with others in activism and become leaders. Organizations can select to focus on one of these tasks over the other and these decisions can have important implications for both the group and its members. The Portland activists were very successful at mobilizing but were less adept at, and perhaps less interested in, organizing. This had important implications for their ability to wage events and support organizations over time.

Research shows that groups that are the most successful do both mobilizing and organizing (Han, 2014). In this chapter, I examine how groups across the ten cities worked to attract and retain their members, focusing on mobilizing and/or organizing. I extend past work by arguing that groups' decisions about which task to focus on, or to focus on both, are related to the context in which they mobilize, and the effect of these different strategies is highly context dependent.

Just as in Portland, I found that liberal cities and cities with larger populations tend to focus on mobilizing, sometimes at the expense of organizing. This strategy was associated with some very large events. Groups in these cities were often able to put most of their energy into mobilizing these large events because they did not need to spend the time and energy to attract new activists or retain their members over time. Groups in these areas also tended to have a more progressive message, as they had less need to work to appeal to people across the political spectrum. However, there were costs to these strategies, as we see in Portland. These groups did not tend to expand activist circles and had higher rates of turnover because there was less focus on retention and easing the burdens of activism.

In smaller or more conservative areas, activists often struggled initially. There were fewer potential recruits to mobilize and more local resistance. However, when leaders in these less conducive contexts were strategic, they could create strong and vibrant organizations. Because the pool of potential activists was smaller, groups had to work harder to find members. They often sought new activists or those outside traditional progressive circles. When groups were successful at this, they could increase the scope of activist communities in their areas. In addition, groups in less conducive areas were also more likely to have members who sustained their engagement because these groups focused more on retention, making engagement fun and sustainable for people with work and family responsibilities. In essence, some groups in the smaller and more conservative areas were able to very effectively mount campaigns because they were focused initially on organizing and turned only later to mobilizing. How organizations mobilize and organize is the focus of this chapter. Through comparisons of groups across the ten cities in this study, we can see how these decisions, and the results of these decisions, differ across contexts.

Mobilizing across Contexts: Targeting Activists

The process of mobilizing and organizing begins with micro-mobilization, "the range of interactive processes devised and employed by SMOs and their representative actors to mobilize or influence various target groups with respect to the pursuit of collective or common interests" (Snow et al., 1986, p. 465). Micro-mobilization is a multistage process (Klandermans, 1984; Klandermans and Oegema, 1987; Schussman and Soule, 2005; Viterna, 2013; Ward, 2016). While individuals make decisions to engage in activism, they do so within complex interactional and organizational contexts (Han, 2014). This chapter focuses on these decisions within organizations, highlighting how activists have agency in selecting strategies across contexts.

The first step in the mobilization process is to delineate the population from which the group is seeking participants. Simply seeking new recruits from a given population certainly does not guarantee that the group will be successful in mobilizing from this group. However, not attempting to recruit from some population makes it much less likely that they will become members of one's organization. Klandermans and Oegema call this initial step the formation of mobilizing potentials, the people who could be mobilized by SMOs (1987; see also Oegema and Klandermans, 1994). This group includes those who have a positive opinion toward a movement and are sympathetic to both the means and goals of the group. The boundaries within which a recruitment campaign may succeed are delimited by the mobilization potential (Klandermans and Oegema, 1987), making its demarcation a crucial first step in the multistage mobilization process (Kriesi, Saris, and Wille, 1993). While this is clearly an important step, research has tended to begin by looking at how groups mobilize members, not how they decide whom to mobilize. I argue that this initial step of delineating the mobilizing potential is critical for groups and has important implications for group outcomes.

The Indivisible groups across the country differed greatly in how they delineated the mobilization potential. First, groups in this study identified different scopes of mobilization, from only focusing on people who are very progressive or leftist to attempting to mobilize across the political spectrum, including attempting to attract disenfranchised Republicans or Independents. Groups also differed in the extent to which they focused on individuals who are already activists or attempted to mobilize those new to political engagement. There are many reasons why a group might have a smaller and more focused recruitment scope, concentrating on progressives who are already activists instead of a larger and more encompassing group. I begin by examining the reasons why groups chose these different scopes of mobilization potential and the impact these decisions have on the characteristics of their group and group outcomes. I also examine how the political context of the area, including its political ideological leaning and history of activism, shaped the propensity of groups to select broader or more narrow mobilization potentials.

Progressives, Independents, and Indignants

Indivisible, at the national level, is not affiliated with the Democratic Party. However, it is focused on a progressive platform and is specifically anti-Trump. This left the local Indivisible groups in this study with options. Most groups responded by focusing exclusively on attracting progressives, explicitly not spending energy to recruit people who were not already Democratic voters. A smaller subset of groups focused mostly on progressives but also sought to attract Independents. Finally, a very small number of local Indivisible organizations intentionally reached out to Republicans or conservatives. The decision about where to focus mobilization attempts was shaped by the political context of the areas in which the activists worked and the pool of potential recruits in those areas.

Most groups in this study (58 percent) never targeted individuals who were not already Democrats and/or progressives. This was particularly true in the larger cities and in areas where there was a long history of activism, such as Portland and Atlanta. In these contexts, it was much easier to limit mobilization attempts to groups of people who are already quite sympathetic to the cause and whose identities already closely aligned with the group. There simply were many more of these people available to the organizers. And this strategy made sense in these contexts. If there are enough progressive activists available, it is much easier to focus on them. First, organizers need to pay less attention to making messages broadly appealing. And, second, there are fewer potential conflicts within the group as members come from more similar ideological positions.

Choosing to eschew mobilizing people outside of very narrow progressive circles was a luxury that was only possible (or possibly successful) in areas where there were enough progressive activists available to mobilize. In areas where there was less history of activism or where the general population was smaller, groups often had to cast their net somewhat wider. It is clear that, even in these areas, progressives and Democrats were the first natural targets of mobilization. However, in these smaller and less activist cities, groups were at least somewhat conscious of not alienating Independents in the process of mobilizing progressives. These groups did not attempt to recruit self-identified Republicans, but they were willing to reach out beyond the classic progressive circles. About one-third of the organizations in this study used this strategy (34 percent). These groups were less likely to explicitly label themselves as aligned with the Democratic Party although, to my knowledge, they only endorsed Democratic candidates when they did engage in this sort of explicit political support. However, they did not put information explicitly linked to the Democratic Party on their Facebook pages or cooperate with the Democratic Party at their events. This strategy was much more likely in areas that were majority Republican or where the electorate was politically mixed. However, it was also more likely to occur in areas with populations that were sufficiently large and where there were potential activists from different political backgrounds from which to recruit. Even in areas that were heavily Republican, if the population was large enough, there could still be a sufficiently large base of recruitment to focus on already-sympathetic potential activists.

Pittsburgh 4 illustrates the careful way that groups negotiated decisions about who to recruit in a large city with a politically mixed population. Donna begins by describing Pittsburgh 4 as "very partisan. We are not Republican. We're not reaching out. We're not reaching out to our conservative Republican brethren saying, 'Come join our group.' We are actively working against the Republican agenda." However, she quickly adds that "we have reached out and gotten more Independents and more people who I wouldn't have thought would come to a march. They have started to come to these marches." This seems to be the result of the group's work to attract both Independents and "reformed past Republicans."

The leaders of Pittsburgh 4 also showed a consistent interest in expanding ideologically by working with nonpartisan organizations in their community. As Michelle explains, "We're partnering with another group that some of us attend the meetings of. They're out of Philadelphia, but they are starting local chapters, and they are very focused on corruption in Harrisburg. They're nonpartisan, but they want to get legislation passed to ban corruption from lobbyists." Pittsburgh 4 illustrates how groups can self-label as progressive but not align with the Democratic Party in order to attract a somewhat larger ideological mobilization potential. This larger delineation enables the group to also attract Independents and sometimes "past" Republicans, but it mostly excludes current Republicans or those who are active Trump supporters.

A final, much smaller, set of organizations (9 percent) explicitly label themselves nonpartisan and actively worked to attract Republicans, sometimes even intentionally distancing themselves from the

Democratic Party in the process. The Salt Lake City groups were the clearest illustration of this strategy (particularly Salt Lake City 2 and Salt Lake City 3). Amarillo 1 encompassed a mix of activists, some of whom embraced this strategy while others did not. These are both smaller cities located within conservative states. They did not have extensive pools of activists from which to draw and, as a result, were motivated to reach out to larger groups of potential recruits.

The Salt Lake City 3 organizers cast a broad net for potential new recruits. They sought to mobilize Democrats, Republicans, and Independents and were also attuned to mobilizing the large group of Mormons in the state. The unique context of Salt Lake City, with a relatively small population and a conservative political landscape (at least at the state level), meant that there were fewer people who had been traditional long-term progressive activists. The people who began the Indivisible organizations in the city were politically diverse and had less activist experience. These varied backgrounds made them more sensitive to how to attract others like themselves who were new to progressive politics.

There were two main leaders in Salt Lake City 3. Michael was new to political engagement and used to be a registered Republican. Stefanie describes herself as "apolitical." She explains,

> If any other Republican had been elected as president, I would not have gotten involved in this. I am not in this primarily for any particular policy reason. I'm in it because I feel like the institutions that underlie our democracy are being attacked, the rule of law is being attacked, basically respect and civility and decency towards other human beings are being attacked, and this is going to have ripples throughout our country, that is going to damage our country. That's why I'm involved.

Stefanie is careful to explain that she is not a "left-wing nutcase." Her identification as a nonpolitical person informs both her personal activism as well as the activities of Salt Lake City 3, in which she is a co-leader.

There were many reasons why organizers in Salt Lake City felt that certain former Republicans could be mobilized to the group. Some group members pointed to the results of the 2016 election in Utah as an indication of underlying anti-Trump sentiment in the conservative state. Trump won Utah, but a third-party candidate, Evan McMullin, also received a relatively large percentage of the vote. The vote breakdown in the state was Donald Trump at 45 percent, Hillary Clinton at 27 percent, and Evan McMullin at 21 percent. Clearly there was not strong support for Clinton as the Democratic candidate. However, it is equally apparent that many voters in Utah were also not supporters of Trump, selecting the third-party candidate. Salt Lake City 3 identified this group of people as mobilizable and strategized around recruiting them. As Patrick explains, "I think everyone who voted for Evan McMullin is a friend of [Salt Lake City 3]. Those are the conservatives that get it." And, in general, the group argued that "the last election does show that maybe you're not going to turn everyone super blue, but definitely people have room to move more into the center" (Patrick, Salt Lake City 3).

Salt Lake City 3 spent considerable energy working to frame its activities in a way that was sensitive to the political context of the state and aimed at recruiting a broader ideological range of people. As Stefanie explains, Utah

is pretty obviously a deeply red state, deeply conservative, and if we were seen as a Democratic organization we would lose all credibility among moderate Republicans who dislike Trump. We thought there are some Republicans out here who really are in agreement with us when we talk about the assault on civility and respect for different kinds of people, and the respect for institutions and the rule of law. Those issues really cross partisan lines, and we don't want to lose those people by labeling ourselves a Democratic organization because the word "Democrat" just turns off the majority of Utahns.

Despite this intentional attempt not to label themselves as a Democratic organization, Stefanie is clear to say that "there's no question but that we're a liberal-leaning organization, and there's no question that most of our membership is Democratic. But we want to leave the door open for moderate Republicans, because they're without a home."

There were a few specific ways that Salt Lake City 3 intentionally reached out to Independents and Republicans. First, issue framing was critical. Michael highlights how focusing on calling the group a "good governance group" and working on issues like gerrymandering and ethics were popular across party lines. Second, the group specifically avoided any partisan activity. As Stefanie, who moderated the Facebook page, explains, she did not post events that were "blatantly partisan." When I asked if this applied to Republican or Democratic events, she responded that the group was especially unlikely to list events that were explicitly Democratic. The desire to distance the group from the Democratic Party was raised by many of the organizers. They explained that this came from a stigma in local politics of being labeled a Democrat. Andrew describes how "a lot of people who want to work for progressive politics stuff aren't willing to register as Democrat just because of the stigma of that in the state. And they don't necessarily want to agree with a lot of the platforms, a lot of the policy platforms the Democratic Party has. So calling ourselves Democrats would not make sense."

The groups in Amarillo also attempted to mobilize Republicans, although this strategy was not universally embraced across the groups in the city. Amarillo 1, in particular, was a very diverse group and was interested in reaching beyond traditional Democratic politics. As Melissa explains, there were some people in the group who

just wanted to let [the public] know that there was a more liberal set of individuals in Amarillo, and that you didn't have to necessarily be labeled as a Democrat in order to have a place to go and express your views. You could be a disenfranchised Republican, you could be an Independent, you could be whatever it is you were, Indivisible was kind of that place that was nonpartisan and unlabeled.

The group works hard, Melissa explains, "to keep it nonpartisan because again, we want it to be a haven for people who just may not agree with what the Republican Party was doing at that point."

However, Amarillo 2, situated in the same political context, engaged in a very different strategy. Barbara, who was active in the group, acknowledges that it is important not to be seen as too radical for fear of alienating potential members. However, she also explained that

> we are partisan here. We are the underdogs. We're the outcasts, and if we don't do what we do, who else is going to do it? That's kind of what I think the majority of the members did. So, I think we're definitely a partisan group. Democratic, Liberal, Independent. I haven't met a conservative that is a part of our group, so I'd say we're very partisan. And that's going back to that outcast and underdog role, you know, if we don't do it, who else is going to? And that type of mentality really keeps us going here.

The case of Amarillo makes it clear that the context does not dictate the strategy. Groups consider their context, but then they are active agents in selecting the strategy that makes sense for their group within this context. Amarillo 1 and Amarillo 2 responded to the same context by identifying very different mobilizing potentials. While both groups survived over the two years, Amarillo 1 was able to mobilize many more events, hosting fifty-six events compared to the nine events hosted by Amarillo 2. The group decision about how widely to cast a net for members was clearly a part of explaining its differential success in mobilization in this period.

Long-Timers and First-Timers

Another critical decision that organizers must make when delineating their mobilizing potential is deciding whether to focus on long-time activists or those new to engagement. This decision was sometimes conscious and deliberate, such as when organizers focused their attention on attracting first-time participants. However, much of the time, groups did not intentionally discuss whether to concentrate on new or longtime activists. Instead, this focus was simply a consequence of other decisions the group made, such as what types of events to host and how to describe events on the group Facebook page.

The literature on social movements indicates that those who have already engaged in activism are much more likely to do so again (McAdam, 1986; Taylor et al., 2009). Dana Fisher's work (2019) examines the participants in a series of marches in Washington, DC, in the broader cycle of contention that is the Resistance. She found that the vast majority of participants at these marches had attended more than one protest event in the past five years. For attendees at the Women's March, a full 83 percent had participated in another protest in the preceding five-year period. And, when she compared the earliest marches (such as the Women's March) with the later marches in this series of events (such as the March for Science, People's Climate March, March for Racial Justice, Women's March 2018, March for Our Lives, and Families Belong Together), she found that the people who attended the later marches were very likely to have participated in the earlier protest events. In essence, once a person was activated in this cycle of contention, they were likely to continue to participate, and an increasingly smaller proportion of protesters were "new" in each of the later marches.

Given that those who have already been mobilized are likely to continue to engage over time, it is not surprising that groups would tend to focus their recruitment efforts on people who have already been involved in activism. However, what should an organizer do if they are in an area with fewer people who have already been involved from which to select? The events at the center of Fisher and colleagues' research (2017, 2018, 2019) were in Washington, DC, where there are many local activists from which to draw and a large group of people willing to travel from afar to engage. However, the situation might be quite different in areas of the country with fewer activists. The smaller supply of activists could derive from the fact that an area is more conservative, there is not a long history of activism, the population is small, or it is located where people do not come from afar to engage. In these contexts, organizers are left with only the local selection of recruits from which to mobilize. As a result, looking to new and first-time participants can become a critical part of a group's mobilizing strategy.

The decision to try to mobilize those new to activism comes with challenges. It is difficult to get people who have never been involved to come out to events or to join groups. It often takes considerable energy to mobilize those new to engagement. There are a number of reasons for this. First, they are not already involved in activist circles, so they can be harder to access. Second, they are potentially less open to activist causes or strategies. In areas where there are a lot of potential activists and people who have already engaged, groups often do not focus on attracting new members. The potential pool of recruits is already large without having to spend the additional resources to attract a more challenging group of people who have not already been involved. However, in areas with more limited pools of existing activists, groups were much more likely to spend large amounts of energy to attract new members and maintain the engagement of their members over time.

Groups had a number of techniques to attract new members. One way they did this was by adding information in the description of events online that helped to make activism seem more approachable and signaled that there would be support for those new to engagement. For example, groups explained that they would pair new canvassers with experienced activists, had information events aimed at demystifying complex legislation, or hosted workshops to teach people how to write a letter to their member of Congress. These groups were also more attuned to the emotional barriers some might feel when first getting involved. There were often comments in the event descriptions about the anxiety that new activists might experience or how to deal with socially awkward situations, such as when confronting a hostile neighbor while going door-to-door. These strategies were generally useful in reducing the barriers to participation for all members, as I will discuss in relation to the later stages of mobilization. However, they were particularly important for facilitating the participation of those new to engagement.

The Salt Lake City groups engaged in much work to facilitate first-time activism, in part because they had a smaller pool from which to mobilize. Organizers in Salt Lake City recognized that participating in activism for the first time can be intimidating; people might be concerned about social and political issues but do not know how to *do* activism. A simple call, such as "Interested . . . but don't know how to get involved?" conveys how these groups worked to integrate new activists into their groups (Salt Lake City 1, January 30). Salt Lake City 1 explained, "If you have never lobbied before, don't worry. We will team you up with an experienced person and give you a quick training so you can see just how easy it really is" (February 1). These groups also worked more generally to educate potential activists, such as at an event focused on "taking questions as we help demystify our legislative process" (Salt Lake City 2, May 30). Salt Lake City 2 offered workshops to help teach individuals how to write letters to the editor, phone a member of Congress, write persuasive op-eds, and support petitions.

The Salt Lake City groups considered the emotional challenges that first-time activists might face, such as the anxiety and socially awkward situations that they might encounter in the course of engagement. At one event, they explained, "We'll start with a training and end with a debriefing of our experience knocking on doors and talking to voters" (Salt Lake City 2, April 27). Salt Lake City 1 also provided information about how to call a congressperson or senator when experiencing social anxiety (Salt Lake City 1, April 27).

Many other groups were also concerned with reducing barriers to participation for their members. However, groups in small cities and more conservative areas were much more likely to focus on trying to attract new activists. In order to mobilize a large event, or even have an organization that could sustain itself over time, the Indivisible groups in these areas had to look outside of the regular activist networks to both people who had not been involved or those who did not traditionally see themselves as politically on the left. Delineating a larger mobilization potential, to include these two groups, presented both challenges and opportunities to the organizations. While it is always harder to mobilize those new to activism or those ideologically more distant from the core of a group, in areas with fewer other choices, this could be a strategic way to increase numbers.

Motivating Participation

Once the mobilization potential has been delineated, groups must motivate potential recruits to engage.[1] The motivation to participate is a result of both the perceived costs and benefits of engagement (Klandermans, 1984; Oberschall, 1973). The benefits of engagement can be collective or selective (Olson, 1965). Collective incentives include a variety of benefits that come to the group as a whole, such as group solidarity and a commitment to moral purpose (Gamson and Fireman, 1979; Jenkins, 1982). These types of incentives encourage the individual to see the connections between their own personal interests and the collective good. Movement actors must work to help individuals see these connections, and they do this in a number of different ways.

Groups can create collective incentives by fostering feelings of empowerment and efficacy within the group. These feelings of collective empowerment can help motivate individuals to engage and support their participation over time. As Andrea, in Pasadena 3, explains, "We are looking to empower people. It does not matter why people attend in the first place. Maybe they have something inside them that they're thinking and feeling about what's going on. It's being able to work together, to feel that working together is going to accomplish something." This feeling of collective empowerment comes as members interact with one another within the group.

The creation of feelings of solidarity is also critical for participation (Fantasia, 1988; Taylor et al., 2009). One way that groups can foster feelings of solidarity is through creating an "other" against which the group is fighting. Much research has found that vilifying an enemy can be quite effective at helping groups bond around a common cause, although there are risks to this strategy. As Vanderford explains, vilifying an enemy "unif[ies] individuals in movements, provides a clear target for movement action, and allows activists to define themselves and their position in opposition to those of their adversaries" (1989, p. 166). This can be either personal vilification, when a specific individual is cast as the enemy, or categorical vilification, when an abstract social group is labeled as the "other" (Berger and Luckman, 1967). For example, a group could vilify an individual, such as President Trump, or a group of people, such as the Republican Party as a whole. This allows members to claim the moral high ground and help clarify their own ideological positions by giving them an enemy against which to react.

Personal vilification was differentially used across groups in this study. One way to assess this is to examine the percentage of a group's event descriptions where Trump was specifically mentioned. To do this, I coded if Trump was named in the titles and description of each event. Groups mentioned Trump, on average, in 10.8 percent of their event titles and descriptions. However, there was a large range in this propensity, with 26 percent (nine) of groups never mentioning Trump in any event title or description. Only one group mentioned Trump in more than one-third of their events (mentioning him in 51 percent of their event posts). In many ways, these are surprisingly low numbers, given the general focus of the groups on resisting policies that Trump was supporting and Trump's low approval ratings among group members and the public in this period. It is also interesting to note that the frequency of mentioning Trump specifically did not differ significantly across contexts. In liberal cities, 11.4 percent of the event titles and descriptions mentioned Trump, and in conservative areas, 9.8 percent mentioned Trump.

I examine how naming Trump as a specific target shaped outcomes for both groups and events. There was little effect. At the event level, mentioning Trump specifically did not have any significant effect on the number of people who said they were interested in or going to an event. At the group level, the number of times that Trump was specifically mentioned as a percentage of all events was not related to group mobilization or survival. Vilification as a technique was not effective for groups, in this analysis. However, it is important to note that it was also not detrimental to a group's ability to mobilize the public.

Groups also work to offer their members selective incentives in the hopes that this will increase the benefits of mobilizing. Selective incentives are available only to those who participate. Only those who attend a protest concert get to hear the music and only those who attend the training session learn how to engage in a particular social movement tactic. These selective incentives can be either social (nonmaterial) or nonsocial (material). Research on mobilization has found that social incentives tend to be more important for mobilizing members than material incentives (e.g., Klandermans, 1984; McAdam, 1986). However, it is clear that there are a wide variety of both social and nonsocial incentives that can shape an individual's propensity to engage.

A wide body of research finds that engaging in social movements, and the continuity of engagement over time, is often the result of the social ties that are created within organizations or in the course of activism (Corrigall-Brown, 2012). Social support for participation in movement activities has been shown to have a strong impact on both initial engagement and the longevity of participation across multiple forms of activism (Maton, 2008; McAdam, 1986; Nepstad, 2004; Oegema and Klandermans, 1994; Passy and Giugni, 2001). And, once engaged, having more contact among members has been shown to support long-term participation (Barkan, Cohn, and Whitaker, 1995; Cohn, Barkan, and Halteman, 2003; Corrigall-Brown, 2012; Houston and Todd, 2013; Knoke, 1988).

There are two main ways to examine social contact within groups in this analysis. First, we can compare the amount of face-to-face activities hosted by a group and examine how this affects group outcomes. Face-to-face activities include events such as street protests, town halls, or organizational meetings. Events that do not require face-to-face contact include a variety of online activities, such as signing online petitions, or attending Facebook live events, as well as activities one can engage in alone, such as sending postcards (Earl and Kimport, 2011). Second, we can further refine the analysis by comparing groups that have in-person organizational meetings with those that do not. Meetings bring members together, face-to-face, to foster social ties and identity development.

The majority of events (72 percent) that groups hosted in this analysis were face-to-face. However, there was a wide range in the percentage of face-to-face events hosted by the various groups, ranging from 10 percent to 92 percent of a group's events. As shown in table 4.1, there is a strong and positive correlation between the percentage of events a group hosts that are face-to-face and both the number of total events hosted by the group in the first two years (0.6137, p = 0.0217) and its chance to survive until the end of year 2 (0.5732, p = 0.0316). The more often a group meets face-to-face, the better their mobilizing and survival outcomes. Groups that have more events that are not face-to face, including online petition signing, virtual town halls, or Facebook live conferences, are less likely to survive or mobilize over time.

These findings support the larger body of research that shows that online mobilizing can be more difficult to sustain over time. This is, in part, because of its lack of copresence, the need to be face-to-face at the same place and time (Earl and Kimport, 2011). Copresence is important for a number of reasons. First, meeting face-to-face helps members create social ties, which support continued engagement over time. Second, meeting with other activists face-to-face can support activist and group identities, which are critical for ongoing participation (Corrigall-Brown, 2012). Online engagement, and both its challenges and possibilities, is discussed in more detail in chapter 5.

TABLE 4.1. Characteristics of Group Events and Group Outcomes

	Event (Number)	Survival (Y/N)	Attendees at 2+ Events (Percent)
Face-to-Face Tactics (Percent)	0.6137 (0.0217)	0.5732 (0.0316)	0.3224 (0.0497)
Meetings (Y/N)	−0.1282 (0.4843)	0.4488 (0.0100)	0.1095 (0.1032)
Training (Y/N)	0.3653 (0.1073)	0.2239 (0.2181)	0.4224 (0.0323)

Note: Numbers in parentheses are p values.

Many of the activists interviewed emphasized the importance of making social connections within the group. These face-to-face contacts help to support feelings of community and solidarity. Michael explains how critical this was to mobilizing in his group, Salt Lake City 3. "We always say, 'you join for the cause and you stay for the community.' So, it's everything we do. I mean, it's a topic every time we meet." Nancy (Pittsburgh 3) also highlights the importance of face-to-face social events, such as potlucks. At these potlucks, "we all get together and create more of a sense of community and solidarity and comfort at a time when everybody was afraid." Stefanie developed a whole new group of friends within Salt Lake City 3. She describes this as "lovely for me. It's just opening up circles, and it was really nice at this stage of the game to just be meeting new people."

Face-to-face events were important for creating social ties, but they were also fun. Many activists talked about the simple pleasure of engaging. As Michael explains, "We always tried to make it fun. We put together people who enjoyed being together. We were incorporating social events and it just became fun. It was one of the reasons why it was successful, it got out that people were having fun doing it and that it was a very low-effort kind of thing" (Salt Lake City 3). Event planning often focused on how to maximize participant enjoyment. Debbie describes an event called "Ocean's 18." This political event was a take-off on the popular *Ocean's Eleven* movies. There were "food and drink and fun and games." The fun framing and atmosphere of the event brought over 300 activists together and helped to solidify the growth and longevity of the group.

There are a huge variety of events that a group can host face-to-face. An organizational meeting was one type of face-to-face event that was particularly critical for group mobilization and survival. Just over one-third of groups held organizational meetings (37.5 percent). The other groups clearly engaged in organizational planning, but they did this either over email or at the beginning or end of other events. I find that groups that had distinct face-to-face organizational meetings were much more likely to survive over time (0.4488, p = 0.0100) but these meetings were not significantly associated with mobilizing higher numbers of events (−0.1282, p = 0.4843) (see table 4.1).

Group meetings can be critical for survival for two main reasons. First, meetings have important benefits for a group as a whole. They are good opportunities to organize events, plan for future actions, and discuss strategy. Second, meetings provide a variety of important benefits for individual members. These meetings provide a context for participants to actively develop their own political skills and engage in strategic planning (Ganz, 2009; Tesdahl and Speer, 2015). The importance of organizational meetings in this study is consistent with findings from other research. For example, Christens and Speer (2011) found that attendance at meetings increased the likelihood of future participation by approximately 30 percent, a result that held over the five-year duration of their study. However, they did not find the same effect for participation in protest events, noting that many of those in attendance at the large protest do not go on to engage regularly in organizing activities. This suggests that there is something distinct about engagement in organizational meetings, as opposed to general participation across a range of social movement activities, that can motivate sustained individual engagement.[2]

Activists in groups that conducted organizational meetings often talked about the social atmosphere at these meetings. Andrew, in Salt

Lake City 2, describes the meetings as "fantastic. Everyone knows each other. Very social, very friendly and also very welcoming." As Linda (Bridgeport 1) explains, "The in-person meetings were very social and helped us to support each other and catch up with each other. The first couple were getting to know each other, just being amazed by these wonderful women that didn't know one another across the state. Some of us knew each other, but mostly we were getting to know new people." In addition, these meetings laid the groundwork for organizing over time. As Susan, also in Bridgeport 1, remembers, the meetings worked to "make those personal connections, and a lot of that just takes time and it takes work and it takes face-to-face and it takes traveling across the state, and you meeting with people and you know a lot of that boring day-to-day organizational work that doesn't seem quite as glamorous as the big showy rallies, but it's so important." Susan explained that the social ties created through this labor-intensive work of meeting with people was the foundation upon which later mobilizing was built and was critical to their group's success.

It is important to note that not all meetings are social or enjoyable for members. Research shows that meetings, in social movements and elsewhere, can sometimes devolve into long, poorly structured debates where relatively little learning occurs (Baggetta et al., 2012; Polletta, 2002). In these situations, meetings are less likely to foster social ties and develop commitment to the group. In fact, Baggetta, Han, and Andrews (2013) find that leaders from teams that spent a larger proportion of their time in meetings contributed fewer hours to their organizations. In this way, meetings failed to reinforce the social ties and solidarity that provide the foundation for commitment to the group (Leighley, 1996). This research highlights how meetings can have detrimental effects, especially when they are a very large proportion of a group's actions, and how these effects might be disproportionately felt by leaders.

Activists did talk about how meetings could be quite boring and frustrating. As Melodie, in the Pasadena supercoalition, explains, sometimes "you'd go to a meeting and everyone would stand up and be like, 'Hey.

My name is Cindy and I work for the NAACP and we have these events coming up if you'd like to be involved.' Then it would be like an hour and a half and I was like, 'I can't take this anymore!'" However, recognizing that this format was having a negative effect on member enthusiasm and the continuity of individual engagement over time, Melodie's group altered the way it ran its meetings. In fact, the Pasadena supercoalition developed one of the most innovative and effective ways to organize meetings of all the groups in this study. It started each meeting with a short meet-and-greet section where each of the member groups could contribute to the discussion around one targeted idea or issue, such as how to retain volunteers, engage with the local media, or recruit new members. It then broke into smaller working groups based on areas of interest such as homelessness, women's rights, or Deferred Action for Childhood Arrivals (DACA). Finally, the meeting ended with resource sharing and training. These meetings are discussed in more detail in chapter 3 on coalitions. They illustrate how groups could work to adjust their meeting format and style in order to maximize the social and instrumental functions of these meetings. Meetings are an important part of a social movement repertoire and can be very useful for both leader and members if designed to maximize interaction and solidarity.

Engagement in face-to-face actions and meetings provides social selective incentives. However, selective incentives can also be material or nonsocial (Klandermans, 1984; McAdam, 1986; Opp, 1983). One example of nonsocial selective incentives is training. Many of the groups invested considerable time to train members in a variety of tactics, such as voter registration, writing letters to editors, hosting protests, running town halls, or going door-to-door to get out the vote. Past research has highlighted the importance of this type of training within groups. McCarthy and Walker (2004) and Van Dyke and Dixon (2013) focus on the leadership development and movement-relevant skill building that are involved in this training. They find that this type of training is related to sustained member participation over time. In fact, one of the reasons that organizational meetings could be important, beyond the social connections that they foster, is that they help to develop organizational skills among activists. As Tesdahl and Speer explain, "Through the intentional involvement of a wide range of organizing participants, these meetings provide a context for participants to actively develop their own political skills" (2015, p. 50). There is strong support in the literature for the relationship between skill development, leadership capacities, and individual participation (Christens and Speer, 2011; Foster-Fishman, Pierce, and Van Egeren, 2009; Tesdahl and Speer, 2015; Van Dyke and Dixon, 2013).

Training among the groups in this study was not statistically related to how much a group mobilized (0.3653, p = 0.1073) or how likely it was to survive (0.2239, p = 0.2181).[3] However, training is significantly correlated with how many of the group members attended two or more events (compared with those who only attended one event and never returned) (0.4224, p = 0.0323).[4] While the collective incentives and the social selective incentives had benefits for the group as a whole, increasing its survival and mobilization, material selective incentives were more clearly tied to individual engagement over time. Group engagement in face-to-face actions was also statistically related to an individual's propensity to participate in two or more events (compared with only one event), although it is a weaker relationship than the correlation between training and engagement over time.

Training was critical for supporting the engagement of members. As Linda, in Bridgeport 1, recounts, training in their group helped to foster a wide range of skills for their members. "We've done a lot of simple training events like how to write a letter to the editor or how to write an opinion piece and we get some local journalists to lead those. Or how to plan a rally, which we've all become real experts at. How to lobby a legislator, that kind of stuff. Because we just felt like how great would it be if all these women who would love to do these things but just have never been mentored would learn how to become advocates of the issues that they care about." Michael also highlights how the training can help empower members who may feel less skilled at activism. In his group,

Salt Lake City 3, members were trained to work in voter registration drives. As Michael explains,

> We trained over 200 people, and it's like an hour and a half training. I thought it was very good by the end. We did role playing and that kind of thing. And that made people very comfortable. We would have fifty people at the training. And we role played, because especially young people, they just say, "I am not political," or "I don't understand how to do this." But we would empower them and give them the tools to do the voter registration and do it well.

Training fostered skills and efficacy in members that kept them active and engaged over time.

Engaging in training was clearly empowering for members, such as Peter. By the time I interviewed Peter in 2019, he was one of the most active members of Amarillo 1. However, before the election of Donald Trump, Peter had never engaged actively in politics or activism. As he explains, "I always voted, but I never really did anything else. I never got off the sidelines." After the election, he decided he wanted to get involved locally and found a post on Facebook for a local Indivisible event. At this event, he was invited by one of the leaders of Amarillo 1 to attend a group meeting with a training session. The training focused on registering voters and supporting local candidates. Peter found this training "inspiring. And it really helped me see how I could get involved." He continued to engage in the group as a supporting member, slowly becoming more active over time. A year later, when Beto O'Rourke came to Amarillo, Peter put his training to use and was instrumental in organizing the events that Amarillo 1 hosted in support of O'Rourke's campaign. Peter explains how the training was pivotal for him: "without the earlier training, I am not sure I would have stepped up to lead the planning for those events. It made me feel like I could really do it, take it on myself. And I saw other people in the group who also were really empowered by the training."

TABLE 4.2. QCA with Outcome of BLM Event in May or June 2020

	Raw Coverage	Unique Coverage	Consistency
WOMEN*RACE*OPEN*TRAINING	0.4	0.4	1
women*race*OPEN* TRAINING	0.2	0.2	1
WOMEN*race*open *TRAINING	0.2	0.2	1
women*RACE*open *TRAINING	0.2	0.2	1

Uppercase letters indicate the presence of a condition and lowercase letters indicate its absence. An asterisk (*) indicates "and." Consistency is the percentage of the causal configurations with the specific composition that results in the same outcome variable. Coverage is the number of cases for which the configuration is valid.

Training had a long-term effect on mobilization within groups. To illustrate this, I investigated the activities of groups in May and June of 2020, about two years after the core of this study was completed. In 2020, the country was being swept by a massive mobilization around issues related to the larger Black Lives Matter (BLM) movement. I conducted a Qualitative Comparative Analysis (QCA) to examine the different configurations of factors that come together and are associated with the Indivisible groups in this study hosting a BLM event in this later period. Table 4.2 presents the QCA and the four routes to hosting a BLM event in May or June of 2020 among the Indivisible groups I studied.

I examined the issue foci of the group, the use of an open Facebook page, and training on later mobilization around BLM.[5] All pathways to hosting a BLM event included the condition of offering training to members, making this a necessary condition for a BLM event in May or June 2020. The most common route to having a BLM event occurred in groups that had open Facebook pages, something discussed in more detail in chapter 5 on online mobilization. These groups brought together a focus on race *and* women. In addition, however, there was a pathway to hosting a BLM event where groups were open and focused on *neither* race nor women. The last two pathways occurred among groups that were closed. These groups focused on *either* women or race. The concluding chapter of this book provides more discussion of how race and gender foci were related to the remobilization of groups around BLM.

The QCA highlights the importance of training within groups. The longer-term effects of this training can be seen when examining the relationship between training and being able to remobilize quickly in response to the massive wave of contention that occurred in the spring of 2020. The groups that were able to do this were groups that had earlier spent the time and resources to train their members. These groups had invested in supporting the development of their members, teaching them to organize events, write op-eds, reach out to other groups, and engage in online activism. By empowering their members, they created a larger and more diffuse group of people who could remobilize quickly. Instead of relying on one or two leaders, these groups had created more leaders and engaged members who could mobilize. This was particularly important in a time such as the shutdowns around the COVID-19 pandemic. Many people were working from home, without child care, at risk of losing their jobs or housing. In these situations, having a smaller number of leaders able to organize makes it less likely that a group could mount an event quickly in response to changing political circumstances. In effect, engaging in training helps to support a stronger abeyance structure (Taylor, 1989) in a group that can be more quickly and easily mobilized.

Overcoming Barriers to Engagement

Movement leaders often struggled with motivating people to continue to engage over time. There is a huge variety of barriers to participation, which have been the focus of much past research (Klandermans and Oegema, 1987; Oegema and Klandermans, 1994; Schussman and Soule, 2005). Participation can be time-consuming and frustrating when campaigns drag on or seem fruitless. It can also be difficult for members to balance activist engagement with other time constraints, such as caring for children or working (Corrigall-Brown, 2012). Indivisible groups in this analysis worked to sustain members' engagement over time by making the act of engaging easier, reducing emotional barriers to participation, and addressing issues of biographical availability. Groups that focused on trying to remove these barriers to action facilitated the engagement of their members over time, which was very important for group survival.

Groups worked to facilitate the ongoing engagement of members by making the act of engaging easier, for example, having scripts for people calling their local officials, postcards and pens at letter writing events, or signs already prepared for the protest. Many events provided scripts for calling elected officials or for canvassing (Salt Lake City 2, June 9, June 14). They also provided free postcards, clipboards, and stamps to facilitate engagement (Salt Lake City 1, February 4). A November 5 "Postcards for America" event listed on Salt Lake City 2's website captures it best:

> We'll have cards, stamps, pens, even colored pencils if you want to get artsy! We recommend voicing your concerns to your member of congress but, hey, we won't object if you write to a friend or even to your mom (or kid). Have an iced drink, eat a tasty homemade pastry, chat awhile, and make a difference. We'll be meeting the first Sunday of each month for the foreseeable future. All are welcome!

As this announcement makes clear, the cost of engagement will be low (they will provide all the materials and advice one needs) and the level of enjoyment will be high (there will be food and jokes). In these ways, the group is making engagement easy and fun.

Another important barrier to action is the negative emotions that can result from engaging. While it is clear that many participants enjoy engagement and experience positive emotions, such as solidarity, feelings of empowerment, and simple joy, engaging can also elicit negative feelings. Many members experienced anxiety, burnout, and frustration. Research has shown that engaging can help to transition negative emotions such as shame and sadness into positive emotions such as pride, hope, and a feeling of accomplishment (Goodwin, Jasper, and Polletta, 2001; Jasper, 2011). The emotions of anger may help activists overcome fear and rational self-interest calculations (Shultziner, 2010, pp. 152–153; Shultziner and Goldberg, 2019). In general, protest "organizers try to arouse emotions to attract new recruits, sustain the commitment and the discipline of those already in a movement, and persuade outsiders" (Jasper, 2011, p. 292).

Organizers in many of the groups were acutely aware of concerns about anxiety, particularly for new activists and those who had little experience engaging in certain social movement tactics. Canvassing door-to-door, for example, can be quite stressful for some participants, and some groups spent considerable time trying to address this issue. For example, the group in Salt Lake City that focused on canvassing (Salt Lake City 3) noted that many participants were apprehensive about engaging in this tactic. As Michael explains, "One of the things I'm proud of is that we got people canvassing who had both never canvassed and really didn't want to, like really averse to the idea of talking to strangers and knocking on doors." The group tried to alleviate this fear by pairing new members with more experienced veteran canvassers, allowing them to observe and learn before they were responsible for talking to their neighbors themselves. "We did that partly by pairing up and putting a reluctant newbie with somebody who was a little bit more experienced or liked canvassing more and trying to make the on ramp to engagement as easy as possible" (Michael, Salt Lake City 3). Organizers would tell new activists, "'Come on. Come with me. You don't have to say a word. You carry the clipboard. You don't have to speak.' And then generally what people find is that they want to speak after all. . . . Later on, they're canvassing regularly and we've had some people who have become super canvassers, who had never canvassed and were really nervous about it" (Michael).

Another significant barrier to engagement is biographical availability. There are a variety of different biographical barriers to activism, such as family responsibilities, work, or demographic factors like age. Research has shown that most activists who disengage do not leave activism because their ideology changes. Instead, it is because they have biographical constraints to participation, such as work or children, that hinder engagement (Beyerlein and Hipp, 2006; Corrigall-Brown, 2012; Mc-Adam, 1986; Snow, Zurcher, and Ekland-Olson, 1980). Groups that are more attuned to the role of biographical availability could counter some of these constraints. As Donna (Pittsburgh 4) explains, the decision of the group to work on postcard campaigns was, in part, a response to the lack of time many activists had to participate. She said, "We produced 400 or 500 postcards over a month or two and mailed them right before the primary. It's these little actions that we're doing that are doable for people who haven't time to give up their life to become a community organizer."

Biographical concerns also often limited the possibility of travel for activism. As Nancy (Pittsburgh 3) describes, her work does not allow her to leave town for actions. However, her group intentionally avoided events that required travel in order to accommodate these concerns. As she explains, "It was important that it be something that didn't involve trips to Washington or regular trips to Harrisburg. I can't do that. I've got a life that doesn't really allow for that. So it had to be something I could do in the evenings at home, or at work between things, that kind of thing." Linda (Bridgeport 1) also notes this concern as she describes how her group selects tactics. "[Sheila], who is a nurse, can't possibly be going to events far away if she wants to keep her job. And we want her in the group, so we pick things that she, and others like her, can actually do." By being sensitive to biographical constraints when selecting tactics, the group is able to facilitate the continued engagement of Sheila and others like her.

Another technique some groups used to encourage sustained engagement was to offer a variety of activities from which members could select. This was effective for those dealing with the biographical constraints to activism. Facebook listings explained, "Can't make it to the Monday sit-in? We will also be conducting a call in" (Salt Lake City 1, January 30) and "If you cannot attend the meeting, please send a polite email" (Salt Lake City 2, August 31). Other listings offered a wide range of modes of engagement: "We'd appreciate for you to spend your lunch break protesting with us, but there are multiple layers of participation! If you can't make the march, you can simply wear black and white in solidarity and/or take part in a spending moratorium from 12 to 12 on 12/12" (Salt Lake City 1, December 12). Some groups got creative about providing other forms of engagement, such as Salt Lake City 2's event where they introduced "resistbot" technology—a website where one can sign up and have a letter sent to one's congressional representative (April 27). In addition, many of the groups' events were livestreamed on Facebook for those who could not attend in person.

Offering multiple modes of engagement was also an effective way to alleviate the concerns of members who had emotional barriers to engagement. For example, many groups had canvassing drives for more outgoing activists but also hosted letter-writing events, which are more palatable for new members and those who are introverted. And some of these groups, such as the Indivisible organizations in Pittsburgh, supported both radical and more mainstream candidates so that members could select which campaign they felt most comfortable with and were inspired to support. Offering diverse channels of engagement and being sensitive to the interests and dispositions of members were critical to maintaining individual engagement over time.

Multiple routes to engagement were also critical to fostering the participation of those who felt anxious engaging in confrontational tactics. Alice, for example, describes how many members of her group were reluctant to go door-to-door. "We needed different kinds of things for different kinds of people. For example, I'm not very good at having doors slammed in my face. I would rather sit at a table of a convention center and register voters" (Pasadena 1). Steve, also in Pasadena 1, agrees when he explains that "different people like different things. Everybody has kind of their wheelhouse and what they're comfortable with." If a group could provide other things to do for members who did not want to engage in confrontational or highly interactive tactics, it was more likely to attract and retain those members over time. Stefanie (Salt Lake

City 3) explains how her group managed to keep one member active despite being an extreme introvert. This member

> felt very strongly about what was going on, that it was wrong, but she just hated calling her member of Congress. She couldn't do voter registration, it just was not her thing because you have to be a little bit out there and pushy to register voters. She came up with the idea of writing postcards to our member of Congress, and keeping just a slow trickle of those going all the time. These volunteers formed a little community, and they sit there for two hours every Sunday afternoon and write these postcards.

Being sensitive to the diversity of ways that members wanted to engage facilitated sustained engagement of members over time. Michael (Salt Lake City 3) summarizes this overall strategy:

> One of the concepts that we arrived at very early on was that we have to offer people of every level of commitment something to do. We have a group that all they do is they meet on Sunday at a coffee shop and write postcards. That level of interaction and confrontation is a one. Because you're only with your friends and no one ever sees you. You don't have to answer questions or anything. Then we have these programs where it's like two minutes a week. And you know, their task is to call a member of Congress and we tell people what are the topics to call on. We even have had workshops where we put the phone numbers in the phone of the Congresspeople and that's all they do. That is maybe a level two. Next is maybe going into a public park and walking up to people. That's like a level four because you're interrupting somebody. Going into a college classroom is maybe a level seven, because you actually have to get up in front of 300 people and you have to be prepared because you have a certain amount of time and you might have to deal with rudeness or questions or whatever. The most intensive kind of advocacy we do is knocking on doors. You go up at dinner time and you knock on a stranger's door

and you campaign for someone. That's like a ten out of ten. You're going to get very few people who want to do that. But we really are all inclusive. There is something for every level.

Groups and organizers that were sensitive to the barriers members faced in their activism, and were proactive in attempting to alleviate these concerns, were much more likely to foster the continued engagement of their members over time.

Conclusion: Lessons on Facilitating Mobilization

There are many steps to becoming an activist and staying involved over time. While the decision to join or leave belongs to the individual, groups can do a variety of things to foster initial engagement and support continued participation over time. Some groups spent much more time on this work of organizing while others were more focused on mobilizing large events. The decision about where to focus group energy had important implications for member participation and group survival.

Groups can do a number of things to motivate individual participation, such as creating selective incentives for engagement. I find social selective incentives to be the most important for predicting mobilization and group survival. For example, groups that had face-to-face interaction at more of their events tended to host more events overall and were more likely to survive over time. These events help support engagement by fostering social ties and collective identities that sustained continued participation.

Material, nonsocial, selective incentives were also offered in groups. For example, training is a selective incentive that is not based on social ties. This incentive was not related to group outcomes, such as mobilization or survival. However, training was significantly related to the propensity of individuals to attend multiple events. In addition, groups that had training were much more likely to be able to remobilize later when the BLM movement was widespread in 2020. While social selective incentives supported the overall health and survival of groups, nonmaterial selective incentives were critical for shaping the continuity of individual participation and the ability of groups to remobilize.

Group leaders make decisions about who to recruit and how to encourage their engagement over time. However, they make these decisions within local contexts that shape the options available to them. On the surface, there are clear benefits to organizing in large, progressive cities such as Atlanta and Portland. These cities have a large pool of potential members from which to recruit as there are more people who have previously been active in social movements and who share the groups' ideology and goals. Because groups in these areas have such a large pool of potential recruits, they can create highly targeted messages that resonate with a narrower, progressive Democratic audience. They also do not have to spend time motivating those new to engagement, who are often harder to recruit, or reducing the barriers to engagement for those involved. Because they can simply find new activists if their members leave, they have the luxury of being able to spend more of their time and resources on collective actions instead of on member recruitment and retention. In essence, they can focus on mobilizing instead of organizing. However, these benefits also come with costs. The narrower and more progressive messages that are resonant with existing activists can be alienating to those outside these progressive circles. As a result, these groups are often less likely to recruit new activists, particularly those with different ideological leanings. And, because the groups tend to spend less time on member retention, they are also less likely to sustain the engagement of their members over time, seeing higher levels of turnover in their groups.

In smaller and more conservative areas, groups often initially struggled to find members. They needed to be more adept at creating broader and more generally appealing messages. While this sometimes frustrated activists who felt that their messages were being watered down, it also enabled these groups to attract a broader set of members, including Independents and, sometimes, disenchanted Republicans. Groups in these areas were also constantly aware of the small size of their potential pool of recruits. They could not simply rely on recruiting those who had already engaged in progressive activism. As a result, these groups spent a lot of time focusing on encouraging first-time activists and retaining members over time. In this way, they were forced to focus on organizing before they could engage in mobilizing. They also focused on offering selective incentives to their members for engaging, such as training within the group. This required much time and energy within these groups, often taking them away from planning collective actions. However, this energy was well spent. These groups tended to have members stay active longer and had less turnover. While groups benefit in some ways from mobilizing in more progressive and active contexts, less hospitable contexts can motivate groups to innovate and expand their organizing efforts, with positive consequences for groups' outcomes over time.

5

Engaging Online and Offline

From Facebook to the Front Lines

The first Women's March in Pittsburgh was a large and lively affair, bringing over 25,000 people to the streets. Residents of Pittsburgh had many options of ways to engage in progressive activism in the area in the following years, 2017 and 2018. The Indivisible "Find Your Local Group" tool listed five Indivisible groups in the city, all of which had links to Facebook pages, and many other local groups were organizing events and actions.

One group on the Indivisible list was Pittsburgh 1, a group established after the first Women's March to connect the women who had all shared a bus from Pittsburgh to Washington, DC, for the event. If you went to the Facebook page of this group in March of 2018, a little over a year after the initial march, you would see a group that was still fairly active, posting once or twice a week with over 300 members. These posts were mostly focused on sharing information and tended to be unidirectional, with very few comments and interactions among group members. On March 23, 2018, Cindy, one of the Facebook page administrators, posted about the recent March for Our Lives event. She wrote "So proud of our youth!" and posted twelve photos of young people at the march. This post received thirty-four likes and four comments, all positive and supportive. Cindy posted again the next day: "Here's to the KIDS and their energy!" and linked to a YouTube video from the same event. In early April, the Facebook page had two informational posts about animal rights, one encouraging people not to buy rabbits as Easter gifts and another raising money for an environmental charity focused on clean oceans, and an informational video about a local candidate for state representative. The first call to action in this month did not come until April 16, when a notice of a town hall meeting appeared on the page. From March to April 2018, this page was consistently active, with eight posts mostly containing informational links and clips. However, the group rarely called for its members to move from online engagement to face-to-face activism.

New activists could also connect to Pittsburgh 5, an existing labor group that listed itself through the Indivisible "Find Your Local Group" tool. This group was much more active than Pittsburgh 1, with forty-three posts in this same period from March to April 2018. The first post in this period, on March 23, 2018, begins with "Tired of politics as usual? Us too. Here is a list of ways you can make a change!" It then outlines five ways to get involved in the group, including canvassing, text/phone banking, data entry of voter information, website production, event planning, and links to a volunteer website where you can sign up to get involved in any of these tasks. Three days later, the group lists a "Socialist Sprout Picnic Party" with family fun, free food, and childcare. The group also hosted Reproductive Rights Trivia nights, a Medicare open mic, a reading group, and organizational meetings, all of which are repeat events that occur at least twice a month. Each event is the focus of many posts, often with an initial post a week in advance, a post the day before the event, and a follow-up post including pictures of the event after it occurs, showing group members having fun at the actions. The posts on Pittsburgh 5's page are most often calls to action, focusing on motivating members to engage in face-to-face activism. In fact, over 75 percent of the posts specifically called members to participate in protest or other face-to-face activities.

Both Pittsburgh 1 and Pittsburgh 5 had Facebook pages, but the ways that they used those pages differed greatly. Pittsburgh 1 had fewer posts and these posts were mostly informational. The outcome of this strategy was that the group hosted fewer events overall, only fourteen in the two-year period, and had only 23 percent of its members attend events face-to-face. Pittsburgh 5 was much more active, with 135 events in the two-year period. It also had many more calls to action and worked to move members from online to face-to-face activities. This strategy was quite successful as 34 percent of its members engaged in face-to-face actions within this group.

This chapter focuses on the role of social media, particularly Facebook, in social movement activism. Social media is clearly an important tool in the repertoire of action of modern social movements. However, the form and function of social media differ across groups and the decisions of organizers about how to engage with this technology had important consequences for mobilization outcomes.

The Role of Online Activism

The 2017 Women's March brought millions of people to the streets with pink knit hats and protest signs. However, this wave of mobilization also occurred online through social media and organizational websites. The online organizing that preceded and followed the march has been the focus of much research, which highlights the critical role of online tools for this particular wave of contention (Fisher, Dow, and Ray, 2017; McKane and McCammon, 2018). These technologies were invaluable for spreading information about the initial Women's March, including how to travel to Washington, DC, and where to find a local event. After the protest itself, activists founded a diversity of Facebook and other social media groups across the country that often supported, and sometimes displaced, face-to-face activism (Einwohner and Rochford, 2019).

Each of the thirty-five Indivisible groups at the core of this book created a Facebook page. However, as illustrated by the discussion of the Pittsburgh Facebook groups at the beginning of this chapter, the form, content, and purpose of their pages differ widely. Some pages have many members while others only bring together a small group of activists. Some feature lists of events with elaborate descriptions, while others offer sparse information and few details of their activities. Some pages have a group of administrators who actively oversee the site, while others are only occasionally moderated and only by a single person. And some groups are open to everyone who searches for them on Google or another search engine, while others ask a series of questions in an attempt to limit who can see their pages or join their groups. Activists make decisions about how to organize online, and these decisions have important implications for group mobilization and survival over time.

In this chapter, I ask three main questions. First, is the amount of engagement online related to a group's ability to mobilize activists offline? Second, how does the relationship between online and offline mobilization differ across types of groups and events? And, finally, how does the form of the Facebook page and how it is moderated shape group outcomes? Activists have the choice of whether or not to organize on Facebook or other social media platforms and how to set up their pages and content. I argue that these decisions have important implications for a group's ability to mobilize people both online and offline. This chapter highlights the implications of these decisions across contexts.

Understanding Online Activism

Scholars have grappled with how to make sense of online activism. Understanding this phenomenon is complicated by the fact that online engagement is highly varied. This diversity challenges our ability to compare these campaigns with the offline mobilization that both precede and exist alongside it. Earl and Kimport (2011) have delineated four key types of online engagement that highlight this diversity. First, brochureware uses technology to spread information online, but not to invite or to enable participation. Second, e-mobilizations use online tools to facilitate offline protest. Third, online participation includes engagement in online activities such as Internet petitions. Finally, online organizing of e-movements uses online tools to wholly organize movement efforts online (Earl and Kimport, 2011).

The present study focuses on e-mobilizations and online participation through social media. Social media has become a critical mode of modern social movement mobilization. It is "a specific set of internet based networked communication platforms [that] enable the convergence of public and personal communication" (Meikle, 2016, p. 10). Social media is increasingly pervasive around the world and provides low-cost tools for quickly organizing and raising awareness about offline mass protest events (Tufekci, 2017; Tufekci and Wilson, 2012). In this way, social media "must be understood as complementing existing forms of face-to-face gatherings . . . but also as a vehicle for the creation of new forms of proximity and face-to-face interaction" (Gerbaudo, 2012, pp. 12–13). While there is a wide variety of social media platforms, Facebook has been the most widely used by social movements and has received the most scholarly attention (Fung, Gilman, and Shkabatur, 2013; Mercea, 2013; Valenzuela, 2013; Van Laer, 2010).

Just like offline activism, online engagement has informative, expressive, and motivational functions (Avigur-Eshel and Berkovich, 2017). In terms of informational capabilities, online activism allows easy sharing and distribution of information, which is important for facilitating collective action (Tufekci and Freelon, 2013; Valenzuela, 2013). Social media platforms such as Facebook are particularly adept at facilitating information collection and dissemination by all members of the mobilized group, unlike previous Internet platforms that promoted a more hierarchical flow of information from leaders to members (Fung et al., 2013; Valenzuela, 2013). These capabilities make it possible for activists to share information about protest activities and to engage with one another (Mercea, 2013; Valenzuela, 2013; Warren, Sulaiman, and Jaafar, 2014).

The expressive functions of social media allow activists to articulate their views in a public domain that can reach a wide audience (Fung et al., 2013; Valenzuela, 2013). Social media also provides a platform for discussions within the mobilized group as activists can engage with one another and share thoughts and feelings about issues and campaigns (Fung et al., 2013; Mercea, 2013; Valenzuela, 2013; Warren et al., 2014). These sites of interaction can be invaluable for group members by providing support and camaraderie as they engage in activism.

Social media can also be used to motivate people to engage in social movement activity and to encourage activists to remain involved over time (Mercea, 2013; Van Laer, 2010). This may come in the form of online engagement, such as when one changes one's profile picture to include a specific activism banner or when one participates in a Facebook Live event. It can also involve persuading members to take part in offline activities, such as demonstrations or town halls.

Comparing Online and Offline Activism

Online and offline activism share many of the same characteristics, and both function to spread information, facilitate personal expression, and motivate action. And most groups engage in a mix of both these modes of engagement, moving from one to the other and hosting events supported by both online and offline mobilization. However, these modes of engagement have some notable differences. Scholarship on online engagement highlights three key ways that online activism differs from traditional offline social movement participation. First, online activism can dramatically reduce the costs of participating and organizing and, as a result, can increase the coordinating capacity of organizers. Second, the role of copresence is lower, or even eliminated, online. And, finally, the role of organizations is often very different, and much reduced, in an online context. These three key differences between online and offline organizing partly account for the larger reach and capacity of online activism. However, these features are also associated with the potentially reduced capacity of online engagement to foster high levels of commitment and persistence over time.

One of the first heralded features of online engagement is its low cost. Those who were first to embrace online activism trumpeted the idea that many people could engage with little effort, potentially increasing the number of people who could participate and equalizing opportunities for engagement. Activists can quickly and easily share information or participate online through a variety of free platforms, including social media sites like Facebook or Twitter (Earl and Kimport, 2011). The low cost of Internet activism also increases the power and potential of entrepreneurial activists seeking to start new causes or groups (Della Porta and Mosca, 2005; Lobera and Portos, 2020). The Internet can dramatically increase coordination capacity across time and space. As a result, activists from different regions or countries can quickly and easily coordinate. It also allows people to organize protest campaigns on their own or in small groups. All of this can be done with little time and resources.

One of the reasons that the Internet can facilitate widespread coordination is because online engagement does not require copresence, the need to be face-to-face at the same place and time (Earl and Kimport, 2011). Online activism also facilitates the engagement of many groups who have been traditionally less likely to participate because of time or resource constraints. For example, biographical availability is less of an impediment to engagement if activists can participate at the time and place of their choosing. In addition, groups that have rural or low-income activists who were traditionally less likely to engage in copresent activism face fewer obstacles in online engagement.

The fact that online activism does not require copresence has many benefits, including allowing for the engagement of a wider range of people. However, copresence has traditionally been critical for many processes that help sustain engagement, including the development of social ties, collective identity, and a feeling of collective empowerment. Coming together physically can generate emotions that help increase commitment to a cause (Goodwin and Jasper, 2004), and much work has been premised on the idea that the production of collective identity is based on face-to-face interaction and emerges in shared (physical) spaces (Melucci, 1989).

While online participation does not involve face-to-face interactions, some research suggests that it can still be a site for the development of collective identity (Earl and Kimport, 2011; Myers, 1994). Crossley's work (2014) on feminist mobilizations highlights how critical online activism can be for both individuals and the movement. She finds that Facebook, feminist blogs, and other online venues can be sites where women and men discuss feminist issues and engage in interactions that foster the growth of feminist identities. Caren, Jowers, and Gaby's research (2012) among white supremacists also shows how critical online engagement can be for identity development. Activists engaged in online white supremacist communities were able to create a distinct identity and community within these virtual spaces. Clearly online communities can foster collective identities within certain contexts, and research continues to examine how and when this occurs.

Finally, online engagement often differs from traditional face-to-face activism because of its reduced reliance on formal social movement organizations (SMOs). SMOs have traditionally been critical for activism. Organizations help motivate people to participate through selective incentives, plan events in which people can collectively engage, create training grounds for activists, and support abeyance structures by creating a repository for knowledge, members, and resources over time. SMOs can also function as the voices of a movement and can connect movements to political elites, the media, and the public.

Much research on online activism has examined the role of organizations in this new mode of engagement. On the one hand, the fundamental place of SMOs as the primary facilitator of protest could remain unchanged when activism takes place online. SMOs could simply incorporate online capacities that reduce the costs of organizing without fundamentally changing what these SMOs do or how they do it. On the other hand, online activism could be a new form of "organizing without organizers" (Klandermans et al., 2014; Shirky, 2008). This is seen in the online activism that has been pursued largely or completely in the absence of formal organizations, or pursued by a combination of both formal and informal structures shaped in networked organizational forms (Bennett and Segerberg, 2013; Bimber, Flanagin, and Stohl, 2012). Earl and Schussman's study (2003) of the strategic voting movement illustrates the ability of activists to organize without organizations. They found that half of the thirteen activists' sites at the core of their study were run by a single person, with an average of 2.7 organizers per site (2003, p. 160). These websites were created and maintained without larger organizational affiliations by small groups of engaged activists.

Online activism may also differ in its ability for, and perhaps focus on, sustainment. Because of the lack of copresence and the reduced role of organizations, it could be harder to sustain groups and members over time online. The standard model of "power in movement" is based on the idea that the power of social movements is the result of their enduring social challenge (Tarrow, 2011). From this perspective, the consistency of a challenge is one of the most fundamental components of movement success. However, a variety of scholars have argued that online social movements are episodic by nature. Bennett and Fielding (1999), for instance, introduced the idea of online "flash activism" that can gain power through its quick and overwhelming bursts of engagement. Many researchers have illustrated this tendency for rapid mobilization and demobilization online (Earl and Kimport, 2011; Earl and Schussman, 2003). And this fast mobilization in response to key events may not be well suited to sustained activism over time (Harlow and Harp, 2012; Mercea, 2013; Tufekci, 2017).

There is much debate about the relationship between online activism and face-to-face engagement. On the one hand, the low cost and wide reach of online engagement could attract a new group of activists and make it easier for people to engage over time. From this perspective, online engagement could spill over to face-to-face activism. On the other hand, online activism may weaken engagement in offline activities as people embrace "click-tivism" and other forms of low-intensity engagement. It may be encouraging the type of political hobbyism that Hersh (2020) and others warn of, keeping us watching our social media devices instead of moving us onto the streets to create political power.

In general, research has shown that the Internet does not substantially change patterns of political involvement. Instead, it seems to reinforce preexisting structures and inequalities (Lobera and Portos, 2020). And, because online activism is lower cost, often only a subset of those engaged online participate offline. For example, research on MoveOn finds that only 10 to 20 percent of members ever participated in offline activism. Most offline events were attended by a rotating supply of first-time participants rather than a strong core of returning activists (Eaton, 2010, pp. 177–178). This general lack of offline involvement hampered community building efforts in the "real world" while MoveOn's top-down control of its email system prevented members from developing bonds with one another online.

The Importance of Facebook within Indivisible Groups

The role of social media in organizing is complex. While it extends the reach of movement actors and their coordinating capacity, some past research has highlighted its reduced ability to foster strong identity and commitment among members of groups. Despite caveats, the importance of Facebook pages as organizing tools was consistently discussed by the leaders and members of the Indivisible groups at the core of this study. While the groups used these pages to differing extents, they all found them to be a critical part of their organizing. Across the groups, it was clear that mobilizing online was central to how groups facilitated the engagement of their members, attracted attention from the public, and mobilized new people to the cause.

The activists in this study often discussed how effectively Facebook facilitated the sharing of information about issues and events. Linda, a leader of Bridgeport 1, describes how "the Facebook page is really where we do everything. Where we tell people what's going on, where we keep people informed of local events and also national events, where we have conversations." As Peter, in Amarillo 1, explains, "Facebook has given us a platform where we all can just talk about different things online or post different things, or just share different events that are coming up." Nancy, who is active in Pittsburgh 3, told me that she "can't begin to imagine how this would have worked without Facebook. In part because it's so easy to share information and events and have discussions almost like a salon. As a medium, Facebook is the place. It is a virtual bulletin board."

The capacity of Facebook to spread information quickly was also noted by the activists I interviewed. Groups could list an issue or event on their Facebook page and have activists mobilized within a day, something that is much more challenging offline. Debbie, who participates in Pittsburgh, illustrates this speed in her description of organizing a protest event in support of the Affordable Care Act. As she describes,

> One afternoon in 2017, when the House of Representatives voted to kill the Affordable Care Act, I was able to reach 30,000 people to tell them that we were going to have a flash protest at Keith Rothfus's office at 5 p.m. With only a few hours' notice, over 100 people showed up. There was no place to park there were so many people! With Facebook, our group is now able to coordinate very quickly. Tonight, there's going to be a Lights for Liberty event. We were able to get that out to 30,000 people within a few hours.

The reach of Facebook could be further extended when organizers or members linked to other groups and Facebook pages. When this was done in an intentional way, the reach of the Indivisible group could be exponentially increased. The groups in Pittsburgh were actively engaged in extending their capacity to distribute information through linking with other Facebook pages. As Debbie explains:

> What you could do through Facebook is, let's say I have a couple hundred followers and I could post some stuff on my page and my friends could see what I was thinking and what I wanted to do. But if I found another page that maybe had another 400 and I liked it or they let me be a member of it, I could post there. And now instead of my message just hitting my 100, it was hitting 400. To do that 50, 60, 70, 80, or 100 times. Now people could see me and if you brand your message so they know it's going to be pointed, humorous, reliable, and with a logo, you've got an audience, a platform you can communicate with very quickly.

In this way, the "brand" and ideas of the original Indivisible group could be disseminated through a network of Facebook pages to even wider audiences.

Facebook was ideal because it was cheap and easy to use. Many groups also had email lists, but these were cumbersome and difficult to maintain. Some groups tried to ease these problems by relying on services that charged fees. In Pittsburgh, activists in one Indivisible group tried MailChimp to "customize attractive emails that don't get lost in your email feed" (Michelle). However, this was expensive and later the group shifted to using the Facebook applications that allowed similar tailoring without the fees. Many groups had members who were familiar with the Facebook targeting capacities that further facilitated this process. Patrick, in Salt Lake City 3, describes how "Facebook makes it pretty easy. They literally have an interest group that you can target that's called 'people who are very liberal, who respond to political content.' They have it for people who are moderate, who respond to political content. People who are Republican who respond to political content. So, a lot of it was just low-hanging fruit."

Activists were quick to note that they personally had many issues with Facebook and did not like the company as a whole. Michael, from Salt Lake City 3, told me he "loathes" Facebook. Kim, from Pittsburgh, explains that she "knows there's a lot of problems with Facebook and the way that social media in general has been used to create false narratives and division, and so forth, but it's just been a very helpful tool. I'm not sure what we would do if we had to do this some other way." Nancy, in Pittsburgh 3, agrees that the group "hates to be dependent on Facebook because that can be really a problematic thing, but it has been essential."

Facebook was particularly useful given the demographic profile of activists involved in many of the groups, which included mostly older adults. Michael notes this when he explains that "there's nothing [more] effective at organizing people than Facebook, particularly in our demographic. Because older people haven't really fled Facebook as much as younger people, and that's who's in our membership." Younger people have been more likely to leave Facebook for other social media platforms, including Instagram and TikTok. As Kim explains, "It's funny. My kids, who are teens, they don't even understand what the point of Facebook is. Even my son doesn't have a Facebook account." However, the activists who are engaged in these Indivisible groups were already on Facebook and were easier to target in this way. As Kim tells me, "Everybody's on there anyway. They don't have to make an extra click."

The Facebook pages were also important venues for individuals to express ideas, vent their emotions, and provide support for their fellow activists. This was particularly important for activists who were less interested in, or adept at, expressing their views in public, face-to-face venues. As Peter, an organizer in Amarillo 1, notes, "Some individuals are not willing to speak in front of people, but yet, when they get behind a computer, you know, they'll be more inclined to share their ideas." This was most often noted in more conservative areas, where activists may have felt less freedom to express their opinions. Barbara, who lives in Amarillo, Texas, describes how "a lot of [her] friends are conservative Republicans. Facebook gives us an outlet, a safe outlet. One where we can express our ideas, our concerns, whatever it is without having to worry about any type of criticism or ridicule, or anything like that."

Being Indivisible Online and Offline

This chapter is centrally concerned with the relationship between online and offline engagement. How do the Indivisible groups at the core of this study use Facebook to spur online engagement? And how is the activity on a group's Facebook page related to the group's ability to mobilize activists to the streets? I examine the relationship between online and offline activism in two ways. First, I assess the relationship at the group level, seeing how the average number of posts within each Indivisible group is related to the average number of people "going" to the group events. At the group level, there are strong positive correlations between the number of people who post, on average, and the number

TABLE 5.1. Correlations between Average Number of Posts, Interested, and Going, by Group

	Posts	Interested	Going	Events Listed on Facebook	Survival
Posts	—	0.7895 (0.000)	0.7615 (0.000)	0.2041 (0.2468)	0.2507 (0.1982)
Interested	0.7895 (0.000)	—	0.8187 (0.000)	0.4340 (0.0103)	0.1952 (0.3194)
Going	0.7615 (0.000)	0.8187 (0.000)	—	0.4323 (0.0107)	0.2927 (0.1306)
City Number of Events/Population*	0.3479 (0.0438)	0.4586 (0.0064)	0.5601 (0.0006)		

*Based on Count Love data, https://countlove.org/.

of people who later say they are interested in or going to an event. This indicates that groups with more online engagement, in the form of posts on a Facebook page, have more people who then plan to attend an event offline (see table 5.1). These relationships are very strong and significant. It should be noted, however, that this is not necessarily the number of people who actually go to an event, just the number of people who state online that they are going to an event.

Another test of the effect of active pages on Facebook is to examine the relationship between posts and actual participation numbers in local events. To do this, I examine the correlation between posts and the number of events in the city per 1,000 population, as recorded by the Count Love website. This website counts protest events through data collected from newspaper articles. This is a better representation of the number of events and people engaged in contentious politics in a city than simply using the self-reported number of people who plan to go to an event. However, this does not necessarily include less contentious events, such as planning meetings or social events. Additionally, the relationship between posts for one particular group and the larger engagement in a city as a whole is not as tightly linked theoretically. Despite these caveats, these relationships are strong and positive. The more posts on average in the groups in a city, the more events there are in that city (by 1,000 population). This is interesting given that more posts in a group is not associated with more events in that same group; however, the city as a whole benefits from high levels of engagement in online activist communities.

Next, we take a step further and consider how online engagement, in the form of posts, is related to mobilization in the group, in the number of events hosted by the group overall. Table 5.1 shows that the number of posts on the page, on average, is not significantly associated with the number of events listed on the page. This indicates that pages that have a high number of posts and are very active are not necessarily hosting more events, on average. The number of posts is also not related to the chance that a group survives until the end of year 2.

Examining the relationship between online posts and offline engagement at the group level is useful for seeing how a group's online activity shapes its offline engagement. However, in order to more finely assess the ways in which this relationship may be shaped by features of the event or activity, it is necessary to examine these relationships at the event level. To do this, I assess the relationship between the number of posts and the number of people "going" for each event (N = 7,127). I do this while also taking into account the event type, particularly if it is a protest or not, and if the event requires copresence.

Table 5.2 shows the results of a series of linear regression models predicting the number of people who say they are "going" to an event. At the event level, the relationship between posts and the number of people going to an event is complicated by whether the event is a protest and if the event requires copresence. Having more posts is associated with more people "going" to an event if the event is a protest. However, for other types of events, having more posts is not significantly associated with more people saying they are "going."

Events that require copresence, meaning that activists need to be physically in the same place at the same time, benefit from having more online activity in the form of posts. I coded events such as protests, town halls, and organizational meetings as requiring copresence. Events such

TABLE 5.2. Linear Regression Predicting the Number of People "Going" to an Event, by Event

	Model A	Model B	Model C	Model D
Posts	12.69***	0.49	0.90	0.90
	(0.59)	(1.83)	(4.71)	(4.68)
Protest	295.53**	116.66		134.56
	(111.43)	(107.18)		(113.14)
Protest*Post		13.59***		13.67***
		(1.93)		(2.09)
Copresence	−46.65		−62.84	−50.01
	(110.10)		(112.27)	(117.08)
Copresence*Posts			12.300	−0.49
			(4.74)**	(5.09)
Constant	11.23	75.54	109.29	109.34
	(91.88)	(52.30)	(99.70)	(99.08)
R2	0.1354	0.1481	0.1353	0.1477

* $p<0.05$, ** $p<0.01$, *** $p<0.001$.

as film screenings, online petitions, or writing postcards do not require activists to be together in the same space. When an event requires copresence, having more posts is associated with more people saying they were "going." When the event does not require copresence, having more posts is not a predictor of the number of people "going" to an event.

These models also show that the role of the protest variable is more important than the copresence variable. This is clear with Model D in the table, where both interactions are present but only the interaction between protest and posting is significant, and the model with the highest explanatory power is the model with only the interaction of protest and posting.

Variations in How Activists Use Facebook

While it is clear that the Internet provides many useful tools for activists, individuals must effectively use those tools to harness their capabilities. As Cardoso and colleagues (2019) argue, the success of collective action is profoundly linked to the capacities and intentions of the individuals and organizations behind it. Campaigns require leaders and members who work relentlessly to organize events and mobilize people. Without the contribution of these activists, collective action does not happen. While the Internet provides activists with many tools to organize, the extent to which they succeed in practice depends on the capacities and intents of the people using them. To this end, the effect of technology in collective action is "to amplify human forces. Like a lever, technology amplifies people's capacities in the direction of their intentions" (Toyama, 2010, p. 29). These technologies are "implicated in social change at the discretion of human agents" (Boudreau and Robey, 2005, p. 4).

Activists make choices about *how* to use technology. However, past research has not tended to focus on how groups or movements differentially wage technology for group goals. Avigur-Eshel and Berkovich (2017) argue that social movements exhibit different patterns in how they use platforms such as Facebook, by both leaders and activists. These patterns may originate from the lived experience of participants and they have important implications for group outcomes.

All the groups in this study have Facebook pages. However, these pages are very different. One way they differ is simply in their level of activity—in terms of the number of both posts and events. In addition, groups differ in the ways that they use Facebook. I examine how activists make decisions about their Facebook pages and the implications of these decisions for group mobilization and survival. In particular, I assess how both the number of organizers and the open or closed nature of the page shape group outcomes.

Table 5.3 presents the correlations between the number of organizers and various online and offline outcomes for groups. Having more organizers is associated with having, on average, more likes for the Facebook page. It is also associated with having more people on the Facebook page attend events. This "Attenders" variable is a calculation of the number of people who have posted on the page or said they were interested in an event who then also said that they attended an event. In essence, it is a measure of the number of online activists that the group has converted into activists who are "going" to events. Having more organizers is very positive for groups as it is associated with more engagement online and moving more people from online to offline participation.

Groups also differed in their visibility to the public. Some groups have Facebook pages that are "open" and visible to everyone who searches on Facebook or a search engine, such as Google. Other groups restrict those who can see their pages in a variety of ways and are "closed." Twenty percent of the groups in this study required some level of information about individuals before allowing them to view the group's page. This varied from simply having to request access (and allowing the group access to one's own Facebook page before the individual is allowed to see information about the group) to having to answer a series of questions (such as why the person wants to see the page, if they are interested in more information about the group, or where they live).

I find that groups that have open pages have significantly more posts, on average. However, they do not have more followers. This means that the people on open pages are more likely to post than those who are on closed pages, not simply that open pages have more people there to post. The openness of the page seems to create a context in which more members are engaging online by commenting and posting. In addition, open pages have more attenders—people who are active online and who are then converted into offline activists.

Groups select whether to have an open or closed Facebook page. It is clear from the quantitative analysis that there are many benefits to open pages, including generally having more posts and having a higher percentage of members who also engage offline. Despite these outcomes, there are a variety of reasons why groups selected to be closed. From an organizational perspective, it was useful to have a closed site (or a companion closed site) where organizers could share information and brainstorm away from public eyes. In addition, concerns about trolls who post negative comments on the page and otherwise stymie the work of the group were central to many groups' decisions to create closed pages. Both groups in Amarillo faced these issues, and one of the groups decided to create a closed page. As Peter explains, "We ask a couple of

TABLE 5.3. Correlations between Number of Organizers, Open Status of Facebook Page and Outcomes, by Group

	Likes	Posts	Followers	Attenders	Events	Survival
Organizers	0.5058	0.1617	0.0030	0.3327	0.0458	0.0622
	(0.0122)	(0.4021)	(0.9874)	(0.0724)	(0.8134)	(0.7441)
Open	0.0412	0.3251	−0.0466	0.3165	−0.0462	0.2076
	(0.7123)	(0.0793)	(0.8034)	(0.0828)	(0.8083)	(0.2624)

Note: Numbers in parentheses are p-values.

questions before we can accept that somebody is part of our organization. It ensures that the people who are signing up are with us, not against us, so to speak" (Amarillo 1).

Concerns about online harassment were often mentioned among the Salt Lake City organizers. In fact, Salt Lake City 3 began as a closed group. As Stefanie explains, "I thought it was important to have a closed group so we wouldn't get a lot of trolls." The two founding organizers started by each inviting twenty people to the closed page on the Saturday of a holiday weekend. "By the end of the weekend it was over 400 and we thought, oh my God, now what are we going to do? We've created this monster, how are we going to deal with it?" They brought on a third person who had more experience with Facebook and online organizing. This new addition advised that that they "needed to have a public Facebook page in addition to the closed group because there are a lot of people who won't be in the closed group but who just want to be able to see stuff." At that point, they created a public open page alongside the closed page.

Organizers in Pittsburgh followed a similar trajectory. They began with a private page in order to create "a safe place for people to communicate with each other" (Michelle). However, over time, the organizers realized that "by having a private page we had to really know the person and invite them into the group. We discovered we wanted a broader reach. People who maybe wouldn't necessarily be motivated to join a private page but there might be content they are interested in." While it is clear that there is additional risk in having an open page, because it increases the chances of trolls and public scrutiny, some groups deem that it was worth this risk to increase visibility. However, like the Salt Lake City group, they also maintain a private page where they post more sensitive information. While most things appear on both pages, "some of the more in-depth articles and stuff that maybe only people who are really wonky will want to read, we'll put that on the private page instead of the public page" (Michelle).

Activists across groups emphasized the importance of online organizing. While they saw the potential issues that came with using social media in general and Facebook specifically, none of the activists with whom I spoke felt that they could have organized on such a large scale or with such speed without using these technologies. There was also a clear emphasis on the need to combine online and offline organizing. While the campaigns could not have been as successful without the use of online modes of engagement, the activists were clear to note that offline participation was also critical to the success of their groups. As David, active in Atlanta, explains, "You can't necessarily keep all of this together in just an online fashion. The monthly meetings help out. Honestly, we probably should try to maybe meet more often than monthly because just organizing online alone does not keep the energy up." Donna, in Pittsburgh 4, describes how her group started online but felt the need to move offline over time. As she explains, "A lot of the communication happens online. But when we decide we want to do something, we have a couple of meetings in person, which is really a good thing. Because people do not have the time to meet too often in person. But, if we only ever meet online, we would just fade away over time." Creating the balance between online and offline organizing was critical for groups and allowed organizers to harness the unique capabilities and capacities of each mode of engagement.

Conclusion: Making Sense of the Online/Offline Nexus

It is clear that online tools of engagement have had a profound impact on activism in the twenty-first century. However, the specific nature of that impact is still up for debate. I argue that this impact differs across times, places, and groups. In addition, the effects of online technologies are also the product of the capacities and interests of the actual people who use them. These activists and organizers make choices about how and when to use these technologies. And these decisions have important implications for their members and groups.

All of the groups at the core of this study had Facebook pages. But the extent to which they used these pages, the proportion of their activities that occurred on those pages versus face-to-face, and the way that they organized the pages differed greatly. The analysis of the Facebook groups and events shows that there is a strong and positive relationship between the average number of posts on a page and the number of people who self-report that they are going to an event. It is not surprising that online engagement and posting is associated with online intentions of actions, in the form of saying that a person is going to an event. Vibrant pages with more posts can create a feeling of community that then encourages people to indicate that they are attending an event.

We can further illuminate the relationship between number of posts and how many people say they are "going" to events by examining it at the event level. This analysis reveals that posts are important predictors of how many people are "going" to an event only for protest events and events that require copresence. This means that when more people post online about protest events, there are also more people who say they are then going to those events. And, for events that require copresence, such as town halls, or organizational meetings, having more posts is also associated with more people going. When events are not protests or do not require copresence, having more online engagement in the form of posts is not associated with more people saying they will go to the event.

One could imagine just the opposite finding: that the relationship between posting and engaging in events without copresence, such as online events, might be stronger than the relationship between posting and engaging in events that require copresence. In essence, we might expect posting, an online activity, to be more predictive of a person later saying they will engage in other online activities, such as signing an online petition or attending a virtual town hall. Instead, events with many posts encourage people to get out of their chairs and onto the streets, at a protest or other event that requires one to be in the same space with other activists.

Posting online and having a Facebook page with many posts could be creating a stronger sense of community and identity within a group. As a result, when events have many posts, people could feel more pressure to attend an action such as a protest. Protests require people, and the more the better. Activists can support other events without actually "going." One could appreciate a documentary without attending the screening, learn about an issue without listening to a speaker, or support a boycott without attending the kick-off event. But if a person supports the protest, they actually have to go to the event. And because these events require copresence, one's fellow activists will know they were there. This is especially true in smaller groups, such as the Indivisible groups in this study. The protest events might be large, but the bus of activists from your hometown riding together is small. Groups with more active Facebook pages with more posts, and events within these pages with more posts, may simply be more effective at creating the social pressure and solidarity that encourages activists to engage face-to-face.

It is notable that there is not a significant relationship between the number of posts, on average, and the number of events a group hosts or if it survives until the end of year 2. One reason for this could be that groups that have a lot of posting satiate people into feeling that they have engaged in activism without taking the additional step of participating in events offline. Another explanation, however, is that groups that have a lot of posting online may be specializing in online tactics that do not require members to engage in face-to-face events in the same way. If, for example, a group is focused on raising awareness around a particular cause, it may concentrate on encouraging an active Facebook page where people share information about issues, current events, or legislation instead of focusing on offline actions.

One of the core tenets of this book is to highlight the important role that activists and leaders play in shaping the trajectories of their groups. Activists work within contexts that they do not always control. However, they have agency to make choices about how to organize, and these choices often have important implications for their success over time. Two of the key decisions that activists make with their use of social media are selecting how many people will organize or moderate their Facebook page and whether they will have an open or closed page.

Having more organizers in a Facebook group is associated with having more likes for the page, on average. These groups are also more likely to have more attenders—people who participate online who also go to face-to-face events. Social ties and connections are one of the main reasons people engage in activism. Having more organizers means that there are more points of connection between the average member and the "leaders" of the group. This could increase the feelings of commitment and connection to the group as a whole and get more people engaged and at events.

Groups that are open are also more likely to have more posts, on average, that those that are closed. This is interesting, given that the open pages do not have more followers on average. Instead, a higher proportion of their members are posting on the page. Creating a page that is open might signal something to group members, suggesting that the group is more focused on mobilizing, as it is viewable by the public. Closed pages, while necessary in many situations, might signal to members that they are not expected to engage in events offline in the same way. These pages might function more as information hubs or as places to express ideas or experiences for a group of likeminded people. While the organizers for the closed groups may have made these decisions intentionally with these outcomes in mind, it is clear that these decisions had important implications for groups and their mobilization potentials.

6

Keeping the Grassroots Movement Alive

How Activists Can Continue to Mobilize

The Resistance is a widespread collection of groups and causes brought together to challenge President Trump and his agenda. The term highlights the connections between the many groups involved in this wave of contention as well and with Resistance movements throughout history. However, this umbrella term can obscure the vast differences that exist among these groups. Being a part of the Resistance in Amarillo, Texas, or Salt Lake City, Utah, is quite different from resisting in Pittsburgh, Pennsylvania, or Atlanta, Georgia. This book is centrally concerned with how activists make strategic decisions and how these decisions can be shaped by the local contexts in which they organize.

Pittsburgh 3 is a large progressive group in the city that was founded after the first Women's March. It was a key member of the larger supercoalition that arose in the city as a whole. The group is made up of mostly professional women. The members and leaders' financial, educational, and social resources were critical in the early organizing and allowed them to develop a very effective set of Facebook pages, some of which were open to attract the public while others were closed to enable organizing and strategizing among the leaders of the group.

Pittsburgh 3 was explicitly political and activist. Events were described in a way that tied them to larger issues of social justice and other local groups and causes. Instead of focusing on bridging party lines, the group was unambiguous about targeting elected officials, including Trump and local politicians, with whom it vigorously disagreed. Event descriptions, such as the one for the February 28, 2017, Resistance Address, illustrate this. As the Facebook page describes, "This Tuesday, Trump will address the full Congress with a speech written by so-called 'alt-right' White House advisor Stephen Miller—the man who helped draft the Muslim ban. We already know that his plans include a discriminatory agenda that puts profits before people's health, undermines equality and damages our environment. These plans don't represent the American people, and the resistance is STRONG."

Amarillo 1 is also a part of the Resistance and was founded as an Indivisible group. However, it differs from Pittsburgh 3 in a number of ways. Most notable, Amarillo 1 is one of the few groups in this study that self-labeled as nonpartisan. Organizers in this group felt that, in order to appeal most widely to people in their conservative city, they should focus on issues that they saw as bridging the political divide. Issues like good governance and ethics were popular foci in the group as leaders saw them as particularly effective ways to mobilize those new to activism. The group also worked on immigration issues, as Amarillo has a large Latino population that is active and engaged in civic life. Amarillo 1 tried to stay away from things that it saw as too polarizing. As Peter, who was active in the group, explained, "There are certain issues we try not to address, like abortion. We can't win a losing battle, so we don't try to fight those battles."

The descriptions of Amarillo 1's events focus on embracing a diversity of people with different ideological leanings. The March for Unity, Freedom, and Equal Rights, which the group hosted on April 14, 2018, is an example of this. The Facebook description explained:

> We are marching to resist the division threatening our nation and city, and we are coming together around issues of equal rights and freedoms for all. The current political climate seeks to divide us and to confuse our values. We resist. We march in opposition to chaos and abuse. But more than only opposition, we march as a public statement of support for the values we hold dear, which include standing together and caring for ALL our neighbors.

The tone and focus of this description are clearly aimed at bringing in a large breadth of new members and focusing on consensus issues that bridge party lines. This was a constant focus for Amarillo 1. Facebook event descriptions often noted that the issue at the heart of a particular action was "not a partisan issue." An online petition against President Trump's selection of Betsy DeVos as US Secretary of Education tied this cause to larger consensus values through statements such as "Texans, we can put the party line aside and stand up for our kids" (February 7, 2018). The group was constantly attempting to attract those new to, or with negative feelings toward, activism. Both Amarillo 1 and Pittsburgh 3 use the terms "resistance" or "resist" in their event descriptions. However, they go about their resisting in very different ways across these contexts. This diversity is at the heart of this book. This concluding chapter begins by summarizing the main findings of my research. I then consider what we can learn about what comes next for the Resistance.

Selecting and Changing Tactics

The wave of mobilization at the center of this study started with a protest event, the Women's March, and many of the Indivisible groups continued to engage in protest or other contentious tactics over the two years of this study. Groups also engaged in a variety of electoral tactics, such as lobbying elected officials, holding town halls, and leading voter registration drives. In addition, most groups hosted some less overtly political actions, including social events and conferences.

A huge variety of tactics are available to social movement actors, and groups have agency to determine whether to specialize or use a diversity of tactics and whether to change their tactics over time. Chapter 2 focused on, first, how groups selected the *type* of tactic in which they engaged and the effect of this for group outcomes. In particular, I focused on the use of protest and electoral tactics in comparison with other less political strategies. Second, I assessed the effect of engaging in a *diversity* of tactics or specializing in a smaller set of tactics and how that affected groups over time. And, finally, I examined the effect of having *flexible* or consistent tactics on group outcomes.

In general, I found that groups that engage in more protest and electoral tactics have more events and are more likely to survive over time than groups that use political tactics less often. This suggests that protest and electoral tactics are very successful for groups and help them mobilize members to action. I also found that groups benefit from using a more diverse set of tactics. Employing a larger tactical repertoire enables groups to engage a diversity of members who often have varying interests and levels of comfort with different tactics. For example, a group might encourage more outgoing members to knock on doors or speak at a protest while also engaging more introverted members in letter-writing campaigns or planning conferences.

Some groups came to embrace tactical diversity because of internal features of their organization. For example, groups that allowed members to propose campaigns tended to use a wider diversity of tactics because the broader group of organizers often favored different modes of engagement. Other groups came to engage a diversity of tactics because of external factors. Groups that frequently cooperated with other organizations often came to embrace a wide range of tactics simply because of the tactical choices of their partners. Whatever the impetus for their larger tactical repertoires, groups benefited from engaging in a more diverse set of tactics over time.

Groups also differed in the consistency of their tactical repertoire. The impact of tactical consistency, or using the same tactics over time, is complex. Consistency is statistically related to having more events, but not to group survival. The Qualitative Comparative Analysis (QCA) unpacked this relationship in more depth and showed that there are, in fact, multiple pathways to surviving and that groups can benefit from consistency or flexibility in different contexts. On the one hand, groups using a diversity of tactics and those that changed those tactics over time tended to survive. On the other hand, groups that engaged in high levels of protest and electoral work and were very consistent in their tactics over time were also likely to survive. Thus, flexibility is an important part of one of the routes to group survival and consistency is a component of another route. The QCA highlighted how different configurations of factors combined to create the same outcome.

Consistency was an important route to survival when paired with the use of political tactics. Many groups that remained consistently engaged in political tactics, including protest and activities focused on the electoral process, became committed to these tactics over time. These tactics provided both internal and external benefits. Internally, members enjoyed these events and felt emotionally supported by other members while participating in them. Thus, political activities were popular within groups. These tactics also provided external benefits by offering a face of activism to the community, showing that there were progressive people even within more conservative areas. Finally, groups that engaged in protest, in particular, developed particular types of identities and, as a result, felt committed to the tactics that supported these organizational identities in the eyes of their members, the public, and the media.

Being more flexible in tactical selections was successful when paired with engaging in a wide diversity of tactics. Groups that engaged in this more flexible and diverse repertoire did so for a variety of reasons. First, they could regularly assess the effectiveness of their strategies over time and update their tactics given the efficacy of earlier engagements. Second, these groups were able to respond quickly to larger changes in the political environment, both locally and nationally. And, finally, the leaders in these groups, who were concerned about members burning out and wanted to provide variety and diversity in engagement over time, were able to keep members active and satisfied with their participation.

One of the core arguments of this book is that the local context shapes activist choices and the consequences of these choices. This is certainly the case with tactical selection. I found that in larger and more liberal cities, groups that focused on political tactics and remained consistent were much more likely to survive than those that were less political and changed their tactics over time. In these contexts, there were more activists from which to choose and leaders did not have to constantly evaluate their strategies to attract new members or worry as much about member burnout. The larger social movement sector in these areas also helped groups to specialize and focus on a narrower set of tactics. For example, the groups in Atlanta consistently held protest events over time, even when the political context changed or members left the group because they did not feel efficacious. Groups in this city were working with the knowledge that there was a large pool of activists from which to draw over time and, as a result, tended to be less likely to change their tactics in response to internal or external pressures than similar groups in more conservative cities.

In smaller and more conservative areas, groups that embraced a diversity of tactics and were flexible in their tactical repertoires over time were more likely to survive. In these contexts, with a smaller pool of activists from which to select and a less hospitable environment for mobilization, activists had to be flexible and use stealth in their strategies. Groups also often shifted strategies over time in response to changing political contexts. They tended to select tactics that appeared nonpolitical, such as voter registration or protecting a local park, despite their critical political goals. These strategies were often very effective and worked to normalize activism in these less hospitable contexts.

Working in Coalition

The first Women's March was an informal coalition event bringing together activists who were interested in a wide variety of issues, from women's rights to LGBTQ+ issues, racial equality, immigration, the environment, corruption, and health care. Many of the Indivisible groups founded at this event engaged in coalitions in the years that followed. Working in coalition with other organizations can be a very effective strategy for social movements, and I found that groups that did this more often had larger events, on average, and were more likely to survive over time.

At the same time, not all coalitions are the same—they vary greatly in the breadth and depth of cooperation. I highlight the role of context in determining the form that coalitions take and their relative success. I found that in contexts with longer histories of activism, groups were much more likely to engage in coalitions. And, when they did, they tended to work in a coalition form that I call a "supercoalition." These supercoalitions, deep partnerships that drew upon existing networks of activists and repertoires of action, worked to funnel resources and expertise from newly engaged people to existing groups. Groups working in supercoalitions tended to have more events and were more likely to survive over time.

Groups in areas without long histories of activism engaged in less coalition work, on average, and, as a result, had fewer events and groups that were less likely to survive over time. However, context is not determinative. Some groups in these areas used a specific broad and nonpolitical coalition form that could be quite successful. Context affects the types of coalition partners that groups select. In areas with long histories of activism, Indivisible groups often worked with other political and more progressive groups. In areas with less conducive political contexts, groups that engaged in coalitions generally worked with less political civil society allies. Such partnerships tended to normalize activism in the eyes of the community and potential new members. Thus, while coalitions are generally a very successful strategy, the context shapes the form that these coalitions take.

Coalitions are strategies used by individual groups, but they also shape the mobilization context of cities as a whole. In fact, the correlation between coalition use in a city as a whole and the number of groups that survive in that city is at least twice as strong as the correlation between coalition use by a single group and the number of events that group hosts. Essentially, coalition use can help groups survive, but it also can change the city context as a whole, making it more conducive to group survival in general. In this way, coalitions within a city can change the mobilizing context for all groups and foster a more favorable atmosphere for all groups to mobilize.

Mobilizing and Maintaining Members

Mobilizing members and keeping them active over time are constant concerns for social movement organizations. The process of turning a potential recruit into an activist involves many steps. It begins with a group delineating its mobilizing potential, that is, who will be the target of the group's mobilization attempts. The groups I studied differed in the scope that they defined for mobilization. And, while a group will not necessarily be successful at recruiting everyone it targets, if a group did not target a segment of the population for recruitment, those potential members were certainly less likely to participate in the organization.

The most obvious constituency for mobilization to the Indivisible groups in this study are self-identified progressives or Democratic voters who have already engaged in activism. In larger and more liberal areas, organizations focused on this narrower group of potential recruits because they considered this population a sufficiently large pool from which to mobilize. This was also a relatively easier group to recruit than those who were not already progressive or had not already engaged in activism. Members of this population were known to be sympathetic to the group's cause and ideology and had already been willing to take action.

Some groups sought to mobilize more widely, addressing political Independents, disenchanted Republicans, and those new to activism. This tactic was most common in smaller and more conservative cities. This larger pool was certainly more difficult to mobilize as these new recruits might not share the groups' ideology or be comfortable with activism. However, broadening the scope of recruitment in this way was necessary in order to mobilize a sufficient number of members. Groups in areas with fewer Democrats and seasoned activists needed to work to attract new and more ideologically diverse recruits by making participation easier and more accessible. They did this by offering scripts for phone banking, pairing new recruits with experienced volunteers going door-to-door, or providing training. These groups worked to frame their activities in ways that appealed to broader, and less political, interests and focused on issues such as government ethics, gerrymandering, or increasing citizen engagement, which appealed broadly across party lines.

Once groups attracted participants to their events, they sought to motivate ongoing engagement. Most organizers did this by highlighting the collective incentives of participation. Collective incentives are benefits that come to the group as a whole and are nonexcludable. These incentives include feelings of group solidarity and collective empowerment.

Groups also worked to offer selective incentives, benefits that are available only to those who participate. Some of these selective incentives are social, such as the friendships between members created in the course of participation. Groups that hosted more face-to-face events benefited greatly from the social ties that these activities created. Groups with more face-to-face events, as a percentage of all their events, hosted more events overall and were more likely to survive until the second anniversary march. Town halls, protests, and social gatherings are examples of face-to-face events that support the creation and maintenance of social ties among members and foster collective identities. Groups that focused on events without this face-to-face interaction, such as online conferences, at-home letter-writing campaigns, or online petition signing, were less successful at mobilizing over the two-year period.

Groups also offered nonsocial, or material, selective incentives to their members. One such incentive is training. Groups trained members to engage in specific tactics, such as voter registration or how to host a town hall. These types of selective incentives are not statistically significantly related to group mobilization or survival. Groups that hosted training sessions were not able to mobilize more events and were not more likely to survive over time. However, these types of material selective incentives are related to individual participation. Groups that hosted training sessions for their members had a larger portion of their members attend two or more events. That is, these training sessions decreased the number of activists who attended only one event and never returned to the group. While the collective incentives and the social selective incentives had benefits for the group as a whole, increasing its survival and mobilization, material selective incentives were more clearly tied to individual engagement over time.

The final step in mobilizing members to action is to reduce barriers to participation. Many of the barriers that groups addressed were emotional. Current and potential members felt anxious about participating in some group events. Going up to a stranger's door, participating in a protest where you are visible to passing cars, or speaking up at a town hall are events that could be stressful for some potential activists. Groups that worked to counteract this anxiety tended to be more successful over time. Groups did this by, for example, making sure members could sit together in groups at events and by encouraging members to prepare their questions for the town hall in advance. Offering multiple pathways to participation was also very useful. More outgoing members could speak up at town halls while shier members could make the signs that others would hold. I found that leaders who are strategic in creating options for members were more effective at maintaining the engagement of their members over time.

Online and Offline Engagement

The Internet and social media provide both opportunities and challenges for social movements. These technologies clearly expand the potential reach of activists and enable the engagement of more people at a lower cost. However, they also present obstacles. For example, they require a certain amount of technical skill and create a space where trolls can engage in abuse online. In addition, Facebook, as a company, has many problems that the activists I interviewed were quick to discuss and lament. Yet Facebook was still the most popular platform and the activists I interviewed repeatedly told me that they could not imagine organizing without it. They found it easy to use and they valued the opportunity to interact with members in a space where many people are already engaging for other reasons.

Clearly a social media platform, such as Facebook, is very useful for organizing. However, the relationship between online and offline engagement remains unclear. Does online participation facilitate or usurp engagement in offline settings? Chapter 5 examined the relationship between online and offline activism. It also assessed how groups use Facebook, in particular, to mobilize people to both their screens and the streets.

Online engagement is, in many ways, easier than engaging offline. It can be done at any time or place and it is relatively low cost. However, does online engagement also channel people to participate in face-to-face activism? To answer this question, I examined the relationship between online and offline activism in the Indivisible groups in two ways. First, I assessed the relationship at the group level, seeing how the average number of posts within each Indivisible group is related to the average number of people who say they are going to group events. At the group level, there was a strong positive correlation between the number of people who post, on average, and the number of people who later say they are interested in or going to an event. This indicated that groups with more online engagement, in the form of posts on the Facebook page, had more people who then planned to attend an event offline.

Having a vibrant Facebook page, with many posts and active online engagement, led to more people saying they would attend particular events. However, the posts were not related to the number of events that a group hosted overall. So, while groups with an active online presence were able to get people to attend the events they hosted, they did not, in fact, host more events overall. The number of posts was also not related to the chance that a group survived until the end of year 2.

Groups are situated within cities and all the cities in this analysis had multiple Indivisible groups. In order to consider this larger city context, I examined the relationship between online engagement in the Indivisible groups and the overall amount of mobilization in the city as a whole. To do that, I assessed the correlation between posts and the number of events in the city (by 1,000 population) as recorded by the Count Love website. This website records protest events through data collected from newspaper articles. This is a better representation of the number of events and people engaged in contentious politics in a city than the number of people who reported that they planned to go to an event. However, this number does not necessarily include less contentious activities, such as planning meetings or social events, that are also a core part of mobilization. Despite these caveats, I found that these relationships are strong and positive: the more posts, on average, in the groups in a city, the more events there are in that city (by 1,000 population). This is interesting given that more posts in a group was not associated with more events in that same group. The city as a whole benefited from high levels of engagement in online activist communities even if the specific group did not. Thus, these findings are similar to my findings with respect to coalitions, which showed that coalitions play a stronger role in shaping mobilization in the city as a whole than in shaping outcomes for specific groups.

The relationship between posting and offline engagement is clearly positive and strong. However, the effect of posting on engagement may not be the same across types of events. Is it as beneficial to have many posts about a protest event as it is to have posts about a Facebook Live speaker? To examine this, I assessed the relationship between the number of posts and the number of people "going" for each type of event. In particular, I assessed whether protest events and events that require copresence benefit more from online discussion than other types of actions.

I found that having more posts is associated with more people clicking to indicate they are "going" to an event on Facebook if the event is a protest. However, for other types of events, having more posts was not significantly associated with more people "going." In addition, events that required copresence, meaning that activists had to be physically in the same place at the same time, benefited from having more online activity in the form of posts. Thus the relationship between posts and the number of people going to an event was complicated by whether the event was a protest or if it required copresence. While online engagement is generally good for generating more participation, it was most useful for particular kinds of events and tactics.

Another factor driving whether online organizing benefited particular groups was leaders' interest in, and capabilities with, this technology. The Facebook pages of the Indivisible groups in this study differed dramatically. First, they had very different levels of activity—both in terms of posts and events. In addition, some groups had closed pages, some had open ones, and some had both. And the number of organizers managing the groups' Facebook pages also varied. These decisions had a measurable impact on group outcomes.

Groups that have open pages had significantly more posts on average. However, they did not have more followers overall. This means that the people on open pages are more likely to post than those on closed pages, not simply that open pages have more people there to post. The openness of the page seems to create a context in which more visitors are engaging online by commenting and posting. In addition, open pages have more attenders—people who are active online and who are then converted into offline participants.

Having more organizers moderating the Facebook page was associated with having, on average, more likes. It was also associated with having more of the people on a group's page attend events. This "Attenders" variable was a calculation of the number of people who posted on a group's page or said they were interested in an event who then also said that they are going to an event. In essence, it was a measure of the number of online activists that attend a group event, online or in person. Having more Facebook organizers is useful for groups as it is associated with more engagement online and moving more people from online to offline activities.

The activists in the thirty-five Indivisible groups in this study varied widely in their use of tactics, coalitions, strategies to engage individual participation, and online organizing. The core of this book focused on the consequences of these decisions for group mobilization and survival across local contexts. After the height of the mobilization at the core of this study, many activists and observers who marveled at this wave of contention were left with a lingering question—what happens next?

The Future of Indivisible Groups

The groups in this study all mobilized, for some period of time, after the first Women's March in January 2017. This book examines how and why some groups were able to effectively mobilize and survive over the first two years until the second anniversary march in 2019 while others were not. This two-year time span is a natural place to focus. It included a series of large-scale mobilizations characterized as the Resistance. It saw three Women's Marches, the first protest and two anniversary events. It also included the 2018 midterm elections, which was a focus of organizing for many of these groups. Most groups experienced a lull after these midterm elections as organizations and members reassessed their plans.

Less than one-third of the groups did not survive this two-year period or stopped organizing after the 2018 midterms. What happened to the individuals who composed these groups and the activism in these cities? The answer to this question differs greatly across contexts. In many of the smaller city contexts, activism seems to have ceased and people were no longer politically engaged in other groups or events. Mostly people in these cities had not been active before the first Women's March. And when the Indivisible groups in their areas stopped meeting or did not engage in the type of organizing that sustained engagement over time, these individuals often simply left activism. This tended to happen relatively quickly. Most groups that stopped organizing disappeared within the first six months. Groups that were still active after six months were very likely to make it to at least the second anniversary Women's March two years later. In the larger cities, the death of the groups seemed to channel people into different causes. Because of these additional engagement opportunities, these cities were able to have more intermittent activism: hosting large events sporadically but not really sustaining activism in the middle periods.

Over 70 percent of the groups in this study survived until the second anniversary march. And, just as the leaders and members of the groups in this study had hoped, 2019 was not the end of the wave of contention. The next two years, between the second anniversary march in 2019 and the presidential election in 2020, saw even more mobilization. While the 2017 Women's March was large, the massive Black Lives Matter (BLM) protest events that were to come in 2020 dwarfed these earlier mobilizations.

The roots of BLM extend back much further than the first Women's March. The campaign was founded in 2013 in response to the acquittal of George Zimmerman, who murdered African American teenager Trayvon Martin in 2012. The movement gained national recognition in 2014 following a series of demonstrations in response to the murders of Michael Brown in Ferguson, Missouri, and Eric Garner in New York City. Since these protests, BLM activists have demonstrated against a series of racially motivated murders of Black people, often by police.

BLM protests have been mobilized many times since 2012 to highlight the violence inflicted on Black communities by both the state and society as a whole. Yet 2020 saw a sea change. The brutal murder of George Floyd in 2020, at the hands of a Minneapolis police officer, set off a massive series of protest events in the United States. An estimated fifteen to twenty-six million people participated in these events (Buchanan, Bui, and Patel, 2020). Some argue that this mobilization has been the largest in US history, and individual events were three to five times as large as the Women's March events of January 2017 (Buchanan et al., 2020).

There is a clear overlap between the work of many of the Indivisible groups at the core of this study and the BLM protests that came next. At the height of the BLM protests, in May and June of 2020, nine of the thirty-five groups in this study hosted or sponsored an in-person event, as shown in figure 6.1. This number is relatively large, given that at this same time cities across the United States were in shutdown due to COVID-19. In this context, the barriers to hosting an in-person event were even higher than usual as the health and safety of protesters were at the fore of everyone's mind. Even in these high-stakes circumstances, over a quarter of the groups hosted in-person events. Of these events,

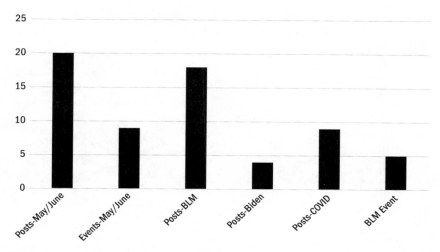

FIGURE 6.1. Indivisible Group Activity, May and June 2020

just over half (five) were focused on BLM specifically. The other events were about a variety of causes, including local elections.

Twenty groups, almost two-thirds of the sample, posted comments in this period online. The vast majority of these posts were about BLM; only two of the groups that posted did not focus on issues related to this cause. Many groups also posted about COVID-19, with nine of the twenty groups who posted discussing the virus and the government response to it. There were very few groups who posted about the Democratic presidential nominee Joe Biden, with only four (11 percent) mentioning him in posts. This is surprising given the strong focus of many of the groups on electoral politics and the high level of activity in these groups around the earlier 2018 midterm elections.

What predicts which groups mobilized in this later period and around which issues they organized? The correlations in table 6.1 present the relationships between the main areas of focus of the groups in the first two years of study, discussed in chapter 1, and various outcomes in the May to June 2020 period, including whether they posted or hosted events and on what topics. These correlations show that groups that focused on

TABLE 6.1. Correlations Predicting Events and Posts, by Area

	Posts in May/June	Events in May/June	BLM Events in May/June	Posts on BLM	Posts on Biden	Posts on COVID
Impeachment	0.3538 (0.0434)	0.2025 (0.2583)	0.2631 (0.1390)	0.3623 (0.0382)	0.1379 (0.5017)	0.2712 (0.1713)
Environment	0.0137 (0.9395)	0.2025 (0.2583)	0.2631 (0.1390)	0.1132 (0.5304)	0.0664 (0.7473)	0.0001 (0.9932)
Immigration	0.1026 (0.5698)	0.1816 (0.3119)	0.1398 (0.4379)	0.1759 (0.3274)	0.3329 (0.0966)	0.1890 (0.3451)
Health	-0.1278 (0.4784)	0.1884 (0.2936)	0.3730 (0.1325)	-0.0602 (0.7393)	-0.0185 (0.9286)	-0.0598 (0.7672)
Women	0.1271 (0.4809)	0.0633 (0.7264)	0.3512 (0.0451)	0.2378 (0.1827)	-0.0533 (0.7959)	-0.0001 (0.9934)
Race	-0.0565 (0.7547)	0.3889 (0.0253)	0.5003 (0.0030)	0.0124 (0.9453)	-0.2081 (0.3077)	-0.1348 (0.5025)
Police	0.1829 (0.3084)	0.1296 (0.4722)	0.2095 (0.2419)	0.2319 (0.1941)	-0.1231 (0.5491)	-0.2000 (0.3172)

impeachment in the first two years were the most likely to post in May to June 2020. And these posts were most likely to be on issues relating to BLM. However, groups that focused on impeachment were not statistically significantly more likely to host events on these issues, just to post about them online. Instead, groups that focused on race were most likely to host an event in this period. And groups that focused on race or women were most likely to host BLM events. It is clear that certain groups were more likely to remobilize at this time as a result of their earlier issue foci in that those with a focus on a related issue were most likely to host events.

Groups that focused on race and women were the most likely to remobilize in this period and host an event related to BLM. Race and women's issues are closely tied in many activist communities. It is not surprising that groups focused on race would mobilize around BLM—this movement was centrally concerned with issues of racial inequality, and groups already focused on these issues would naturally be more likely to connect to this large-scale movement. And groups that have multiple issue foci also seem to be ripe to embrace these issues.

It is interesting, however, that groups that focus exclusively on women's issues were also more likely to mobilize than other groups around BLM. For example, Pittsburgh 5 is almost exclusively focused on women's issues—socialist feminism and reproductive rights—although it also organizes labor events. The group had been consistently active over the four years from the first march up until the BLM events. And, as group members were active, engaged, and organized, they were quickly able to embrace partnerships with BLM activists, issues, and events in their community. This was particularly likely as they saw issues of racial justice as connected to women's rights through a larger lens of equality. Making these larger connections between different types of equality frames created the context that made this mobilization both possible and more likely.

The high levels of mobilization around BLM among the Indivisible groups may appear surprising, given that many of the Indivisible groups in this analysis were composed of mostly white activists. However, it is important to note that this lack of diversity was not the case for all groups. In fact, there were many groups that included large numbers of Latinx activists and other groups that had a mix of racial and ethnic backgrounds. It is also important to note that many of the groups that were mostly white explicitly created coalitions with other more diverse local groups. This was based in an ideological commitment and recognition that activists from diverse backgrounds have unique connections to certain issues. And, through creating diverse ties and coalitions, the Indivisible groups worked to support and not supplant activists already engaged in these causes. This commitment to diverse coalitions was discussed in chapter 3. These connections and coalitions may be why many of the groups that were not diverse themselves were attuned to and able to mobilize around BLM quickly. Engaging with a diversity of activists helped to educate those in less diverse groups about the critical need for mobilization around BLM and the connection between BLM and other causes in which they were already active.

The Lasting Impact of the Resistance

Many groups engaged in activism following the Women's March and through the Resistance came to wonder if their participation had made a difference. This question of impact was a constant and consistent concern among the activists I interviewed. How could they motivate people to stay involved even when the results are difficult to see, at least in the short term? These concerns were manifest in different ways across local areas. In conservative areas, activists wondered how they could change the views of their neighbors who mostly disagreed with their causes. They also felt frustrated by their elected leaders, who were often unresponsive to their claims and saw their issues as fringe concerns. In liberal areas, activists worried that they were simply targeting elected leaders who were already sympathetic and could not change the discourse in other areas of the country where support for their progressive policies was weak.

This book argued that the actions of activists and leaders are critical to the persistence of groups in the face of difficult odds. While groups are affected by their local contexts, activists make strategic decisions about how to respond to these contexts and where best to mobilize their resources. Only through learning from the successes of some groups and the struggles of others can we understand how activism can survive and thrive.

The results of the 2016 election were a crushing disappointment to many of the activists whom I interviewed in this book and whose groups I followed. Activists in progressive areas could not believe that Trump had won, given that their local contexts had vigorously rejected him and his ideas. Those in more conservative cities and towns felt disheartened that their family and friends in their community had supported Trump and his ideals.

Despite this disappointment, activists did not sit back and accept the new political landscape. They quickly organized local marches or chartered buses to take them to the Women's March in Washington, DC, or

New York City. They came home energized and created local groups, some of which were Indivisible groups but also included many other kinds of organizations. And, despite the onslaught of troubling events that were to come over the next two years, most of these groups kept meeting, mobilizing, and planning. And, while some groups petered out over time, many were able to remobilize around the later wave of BLM protests that inspired the country in 2020. The story of these groups, and many others like them, is the story of modern social movements. By understanding their growth and decline, we can make sense of this larger wave of contention and how social movements can thrive across the cities and towns of America.

ACKNOWLEDGMENTS

Activists inspire me. When things go wrong in the world, they don't simply sit home and feel disappointed. Instead, they get out there and fight for what they believe in—a more equitable world, a cleaner environment, social justice. Even when times are hard, which they often are for social movement activists, many continue to organize and mobilize. Sometimes they do this among a large community of like-minded people, working together to mount campaigns or massive protest events. Sometimes they do this on their own or with a friend or two around a kitchen table or café bar. Wherever they find themselves, these activists do not accept the world as it is but see it as it could be. This is inspiring.

My father, Hans Brown, was a lifelong activist. He grew up in the conservative city of Calgary in Canada. He became interested in progressive politics as a teen and, when he went to the University of Calgary in the 1960s, he joined the New Democratic Party club on campus. Over time, he became the president of the club and worked actively to recruit members and campaign on his campus, with mixed success but always a lot of enthusiasm and a steadfast belief in his cause.

When the federal election came in 1965, the national New Democratic Party (NDP) sent a letter to all the university clubs asking them to raise money for the campaign. Hans Brown took up the call. He organized a small group of fellow club members (there were only a few to mobilize!) and they went door-to-door in Calgary to ask for donations. They created the "Five and Dime Club" and asked neighbors if they wanted to join. You could donate either five or ten dollars. They quickly collected $2,000. Seeing the possibilities, they drove up to Edmonton, which was also conservative at the time. They collected an additional $1,000 and sent their bounty off to the federal office. They never heard back.

After my father graduated, he went to Ottawa. He was to interview for a job as the executive assistant to Tommy Douglas, the leader of the NDP at the time. When he got into the interview room, everyone around the table knew of him. He wondered how all these federal party leaders and elected officials would know about a small-town boy from Calgary. It turns out his NDP campus club was the only club across the whole country that had sent in any money to that call for donations the election before. So his check for the $3,000 his club had collected really stood out! He got the job and worked as Tommy Douglas's executive assistant for many years.

When I think of this story, and many others like it from my father's long career in leftist electoral politics and labor organizing, it reminds me of why I find activists so inspirational. Activists like my father are not deterred by contexts that are not as conducive to organizing. Certainly they acknowledge they are hard, but the most successful activism sees these difficulties and then strategizes about how to overcome them. This is the heart of activism.

The activists in this book are just like my father. Some worked in big cities with lots of other people who shared their views. These activists are often able to mount large and dramatic events that bring public and media attention. Those who worked in smaller or more conservative areas had to be nimble and organize in ways that did not bring negative coverage, but still moved their campaigns forward. Some worked to register voters, which appears nonpartisan but helped elect more progressive leaders. Some worked on issues they saw as crossing party lines, such as health care or government accountability, to bring new people into progressive politics. They are all part of the larger story of activism and progressive movements.

My father passed away in 2020. This book is a tribute to him and others like him. People who see the possibilities in the world and who are steadfast in their commitment to making the world more equitable and just. They are not blind to the challenges but look for ways to overcome them. I am deeply grateful to my father and all the activists like him, for all the triumphs we have seen so far and the ones that are yet to come.

I am thankful for the unending support of my mother, also a lifelong activist who embodies the same commitment to community and equity. She is a role model of how we can all work toward the greater good. My husband, Steve Weldon, provides endless support of my work and me. Since our days working in graduate student offices all the way to working at home through COVID, his support has been unwavering. And to our son, Leo, who was born into a world that is filled with challenges but also with opportunities. He has the hopeful eyes of youth. May the world live up to the possibilities that he sees.

I thank my colleagues at the University of British Columbia for their support. And my colleagues and mentors who have helped shape me and my work. I particularly appreciate those who have commented on this book project: Neal Caren, Hank Johnston, David Meyer, David Snow, Sid Tarrow, Rima Wilkes, and Steve Weldon. I also appreciate the excellent work of Ilene Kalish, of New York University Press, for shepherding this project through its review and always providing incisive and constructive feedback. I also thank Sonia Tsuruoka, Alexia Traganas, and Martin Coleman for their assistance with all the stages of bringing this book through editing and production. This research was funded by the Government of Canada through the Social Science and Humanities Research Council. I thank this body and acknowledge the exceptional support that the Canadian government, as well as my university, provides for research.

METHODOLOGICAL APPENDIX

This research involves a diversity of data sources and methods, including Facebook pages that are quantitatively and qualitatively coded, interviews, and newspaper data. Each chapter brings together a combination of these data and methods. This appendix outlines these methods in more detail and supplements the descriptions provided in each chapter.

The study focuses on ten US cities. I chose to examine groups within a city context in order to illuminate the role of the local environment in mobilization. A study of mobilization at the national level, while useful for understanding national processes, would not be able to assess the role of the local context and how this context shapes the decisions of activists and groups. The cities were selected based on population size and region of the country in order to provide a lens on the diversity of contexts in which activists were organizing. Four of the cities have large populations ranging from 300,000 to 640,000, and six have medium-size populations ranging from 140,000 to 200,000. I also selected cities that represented major regions in the United States (East Coast, West Coast, Midwest, and South). The cities are listed in table A.1.

In order to find Indivisible groups in each city, I used the online tool at Indivisible.org where you can "Find Your Local Group." Anyone can go to the website, type in their zip code, state, or group name and search for a local group in their area. I searched for Indivisible groups in each of the cities on February 20, 2017, one month after the first Women's March. This yielded thirty-five groups with Facebook pages in these cities (see table A.2).

I began to collect data from these Facebook pages through automatic computer coding. These data were collected before Facebook began restricting the automatic collection of data from their pages. As a result, I

TABLE A.1. Cities by Political Context and Population Size

	Population Size	
Region	Medium	Large
East Coast	Bridgeport, Connecticut	Pittsburgh, Pennsylvania Newark, New Jersey
West Coast	Pasadena, California Salt Lake City, Utah	Portland, Oregon
Midwest	Dayton, Ohio Springfield, Illinois	
South	Amarillo, Texas	Atlanta, Georgia

was able to automatically computer-code all individuals who attended each event for each group and track the participation of each person based on their unique Facebook user identification number. I collected these data using a Facebook application that the company provides and that enables Facebook to monitor the specific information that I collected to ensure that it complied with their privacy policies. These data allow me to compare the amount and persistence of engagement across the cities and groups. It is important to note that I never collected personal information about the individuals who participated in the Indivisible groups, never went to their personal Facebook pages, and never recorded their names. I also only used these data aggregated by group in order to get an overall profile of the participation of people by group. Facebook changed its policies in 2018 as a result of some very serious privacy complaints from concerned users who were unhappy with the commercial use of their private data. After these events, Facebook no longer allowed even academics to collect data through "scraping." I no longer collected these data after the change in policy.

The next stage of the research involved hand-collecting information on all groups and events listed on each of the Facebook pages from January 2017 to January 2019. This yielded data on over 7,000 events. I coded details of the groups and events, including the name of the event, the tactics used, the number of people interested in or attending, the

TABLE A.2. Mobilization by Political Context

City	Events per 1,000 Population	Mean Attendance	Number of Groups Founded	Group Survival after 2 Years
Dayton	0.17	94	3	33%
Amarillo	0.32	63	2	100%
Springfield	0.36	27	3	100%
Newark	0.41	10	2	50%
Pittsburgh	0.71	143	5	60%
Portland	0.89	179	6	29%
Atlanta	1.22	148	6	100%
Salt Lake City	3.21	160	3	100%
Bridgeport	4.35	140	2	100%
Pasadena	5.46	680	3	66%

number of comments, the coalition partners, the issue focus, the location, the time, and the duration. I also qualitatively coded the description of the event and additional information given in the posting about the event (such as links to additional resources or information). These data enabled me to systematically compare tactics and strategies across the groups.

These data were, in part, used to predict which groups survived until the end of year 1 (January 2018) and the end of year 2 (January 2019). I operationalize survival with two key elements. In order to be coded as still active in January 2018, a group had to have held an event within the last two months and to have at least two comments on its page within the past two months. To be coded as active in January 2019, the same criteria were used for the preceding two months. These groups were coded as "surviving." All groups that were coded as "surviving" far surpassed this threshold, holding more events and having more comments in the time period.

The data were analyzed both quantitatively and qualitatively. I ran statistical analyses to understand the factors that predicted mobilization and survival over time. I also conducted a Qualitative Comparative

Analysis (QCA) in order to understand the multiple pathways to survival in different contexts. QCA techniques are based on Boolean logic (Ragin, 1987). They allow us to consider all possible combinations of theoretically proscribed causal factors and, with its comparative algorithmic logic, eliminate redundant and superfluous information. The benefits of QCA lie in its ability to specify configurations of variables that shape outcomes. Finally, I used NVivo to qualitatively code the description of the event for themes.

The Facebook data collection was supplemented by interviews with twenty-five leaders and activists in the Indivisible groups. These interviews helped me to understand how activists made decisions, the actual experience of participating in the different groups, and the ways that the groups changed over time. They also focused on how the strategic decisions of the activists were (or were not) shaped by their local context. Activists were contacted on Facebook via the Facebook messaging application. They were invited to participate in an interview about their group and their participation in activism. These interviews were qualitatively coded in NVivo for themes and provided additional insight into mobilization across the city and group contexts. Table A.3 provides a list of interview participants, by city. The names listed in this table, as well as in the text of the book, are pseudonyms.

The interviews consisted of six main sections. First, I asked a series of questions about the group, including its founding, tactics, and organization. I then asked questions about the participant's involvement in the group, including their initial engagement and their participation over time. The third section focused on changes in the group as a whole over time. I then asked a series of questions about coalitions and how the group engaged with other organizations in their community. The fifth section of the interview focused on the city context in which the group mobilized. I ended with a series of demographic questions. The full Interview Guide is available at the end of this appendix. Each interview lasted from forty-five minutes to two hours and was transcribed and coded using NVivo 12.

TABLE A.3. Interview Participants, by City and Group

City	Interview Number	Group	Pseudonym
Atlanta	1	Atlanta 1	David
Salt Lake City	2	SLC 3	Stefanie
Salt Lake City	3	SLC 2	Andrew
Bridgeport	4	Bridgeport 1	Susan
Pasadena	5	Pasadena 1	Alice
Pasadena	6	Pasadena 3	Andrea
Dayton	7	Dayton 1	Julia
Bridgeport	8	Bridgeport 1	Linda
Salt Lake City	9	SLC 3	Michael
Amarillo	10	Amarillo 1 and 2	Maria
Amarillo	11	Amarillo 1 and 2	Melissa
Amarillo	12	Amarillo 1	Peter
Pittsburgh	13	Pittsburgh 4	Donna
Salt Lake City	14	SLC 3	Patrick
Amarillo	15	Amarillo 1	Barbara
Pittsburgh	16	Pittsburgh 3	Nancy
Pittsburgh	17	Pittsburgh Supercoalition	Kim
Pittsburgh	18	Pittsburgh Supercoalition	Debbie
Pittsburgh	19	Pittsburgh Supercoalition	Michelle
Pasadena	20	Pasadena 1	Steve
Pasadena	21	Pasadena Supercoalition	Melodie
Pasadena	22	Pasadena 2	Jonathan
Pasadena	23	Pasadena Supercoalition	Anthony
Indivisible Leader	24	Indivisible Head Office	Simon
Indivisible Leader	25	Indivisible Head Office	Samantha

Biographical reconstruction and memory failure are always problems in retrospective interviewing. A number of techniques were employed to protect against these biases. To address the accuracy of recall, I structured my questions around past events rather than past attitudes because memories of events are more reliable (Markus, 1986; Schacter, 1996). In addition, research shows that more salient, less repetitive events are remembered with particular accuracy (Beckett et al., 2000; Scott and

TABLE A.4. Newspaper Data, by City

City	Newspaper	Number of Articles	Number of Codes
Amarillo	Amarillo Globe News	12	163
Atlanta	Atlanta Journal-Constitution	57	643
Bridgeport	Connecticut Post	41	581
Dayton	Dayton Daily News	13	179
Newark	Star-Ledger	27	303
Pasadena	Pasadena Star News	11	135
Pittsburgh	Pittsburgh Post-Gazette	20	239
Portland	Oregonian	25	295
Salt Lake City	Deseret News	68	805
Springfield	State Journal-Register	26	309

Alwin, 1998, p. 114). To this end, I asked respondents about memorable events, such as the midterm elections or the initial Women's March, and then asked if this event had occurred before or after pivotal participation events. This made it possible to assess more clearly the temporal order of events.

Finally, I collected information on the local activist contexts through analysis of newspaper articles in each of the cities. I examined all articles in the main local newspaper from January 1, 2017, until January 30, 2019, with the following key terms: "Women's March," "Indivisible," and the combination of "Trump" and "protest." Each article was coded for the issue focus and the tone of the coverage. I also qualitatively coded for the main themes in protest activity in each area over this period. These data enhanced my overall understanding of the context in which activism took place. Table A.4 provides a list of the newspapers used for each city as well as the number of articles and the number of codes per newspaper.

INTERVIEW GUIDE

I got your name from the website of XXX [group], an Indivisible group in XXX [city]. I am a sociology professor at the University of British Columbia in Vancouver, Canada. My research looks at how people get involved in social movements and what happens to groups over time. I really appreciate you taking the time to talk with me about your experiences in this group.

1: The Group

Can you tell me a bit about [Indivisible group]?

Core issues?

What sort of activities does the group do?

Do you ever protest? Why or why not?

Do you ever do electoral work—like canvassing or lobbying officials? Why or why not?

Do you tend to do mostly the same types of things over time or do you do a lot of different things? Why?

Do you discuss, as a group, what types of tactics to use?

Do you ever say no to a tactic or topic?

How often did the group meet and what are these meetings like?

Did the group ever have training sessions?

What sorts of relationships did you have with people in the movement? (How close/personal, how many people were you friends with?)

How was the group organized?

Are there leaders?

Is it formal/informal?

Is it hierarchical or egalitarian?

How much input or influence did individual members have in the group?

How important do you think the Facebook page is for your group and work?

2: Initial Involvement

Can you tell me about when you got involved in the group and how that happened?

Did you know people in the group when you first got involved?

Had you done this sort of thing before you got in the group?

Can you tell me a bit about what you do in the group?

3: Over Time

Are you still involved with this group?

If no, why not?

If yes, did your participation change over time?

Did it increase or decrease?

Did it become more or less regular?

Did you do different things?

If you did change, why might this be?

Has the group changed over time?

Did it engage in more or less activities?

Did the type of activities change?

Did the people change?

Why might this be?

4: Coalitions

Did your group tend to work with other groups?

If yes, can you tell me about how this happened?

How did they cooperate?

Formally or informally?

How often?

Was it successful, in your opinion? If not, do you have a sense of why not?

5: City

What is activism like in XXX [city]?

Would you describe it as a liberal or conservative context? How might that shape the activism in the city?

Do you get the sense that other groups in the city support the work of your group and other groups like it?

Do you think that the government in your area is supportive of the work of your group and others like it?

Is there a lot of protest in the city? Was there a big Women's March the first year? What about the second year? What about after the midterms?

6: Background Questions

    Age

    Gender

    Education

    Ethnicity

    Marital status

    Children

    Occupation

    Political identification

NOTES

CHAPTER 1. INDIVISIBLE ACROSS CITIES

1   A large population size is operationalized as ranging from 300,000 to 640,000, and a medium population size is operationalized as ranging from 140,000 to 200,000.

2   Any group could list itself through the Indivisible "Find Your Local Group" search tool.

3   From 2017 to 2018, I tracked the participation of each person in each group based on their unique Facebook user identification number (if they were interested but never attended and, if they attended, how many events they participated in within the first year). I collected these data using an application that the company provides and that enables Facebook to monitor the specific information that I collected to ensure it complied with their privacy policies. In 2018, concerned users who were unhappy with the commercial use of their private data prompted Facebook to prevent anyone, including academics, from collecting data through automatic application, such as with the Facebook application I had used. This meant that I could no longer collect the same individual-level data. To my knowledge, I am the only scholar who has systematic Facebook data on participation over time in the Indivisible groups I studied.

4   I only used these data aggregated by group in order to get an overall profile of the participation of group members. In accordance with ethical guidelines, I never collected personal information about the individuals who participated on the Indivisible pages, never went to their personal Facebook pages, and never recorded their names. I also obscure the identities of the groups in this book by referring to them by city name and the number I assigned to them. For example, Salt Lake City's groups were randomly assigned to be Salt Lake City 1, Salt Lake City 2, and Salt Lake City 3.

5   I operationalize "survival" with two key elements. In order to be coded as still active, a group had to have held an event within the last two months and to have at least two comments on its page within the past two months. Groups meeting the standard were coded as "surviving." All groups that were coded as "surviving" far surpassed this threshold, holding more events and having more comments in the time period. More information on this coding can be found in the Methodological Appendix.

6 The data were analyzed both quantitatively and qualitatively. For more information on the methods used, see the Methodological Appendix.

7 There are a number of ways that one could operationalize a city's history of activism. In this analysis, I use a combination of two data sources to quantify the amount of protest in a city over time. First, I use the Dynamics of Collective Action data set (web.stanford.edu/group/collectiveaction/cgi-bin/drupal). These data count protest events based on *New York Times* newspaper coverage. It lists events by date and city and includes events from 1960 to 1995. While the *New York Times* is a national newspaper, it tends to favor coverage of events in New York City and nearby states. In order to more accurately assess the number of protest events in areas of the country further from New York, I also counted events as listed in the *Los Angeles Times* (available through the newspapers.com database). For comparability, I collected coverage from 1960 to 1995. I used these two counts of protest events in each city over this thirty-five-year period and divided this count by the city population size. With these two data points, I found that the number of protest events, as covered in the media, was highest in Atlanta (0.539 events /1,000 people), Bridgeport (0.304/1,000), Pittsburgh (0.303/1,000), Portland (0.258/1,000), and Pasadena (0.225/1,000). It was lower in Newark (0.131/1,000), Springfield (0.130/1,000), Salt Lake City (0.124/1,000), Dayton (0.093/1,000), and Amarillo (0.020/1,000) in the thirty-five-year period.

CHAPTER 2. DECIDING WHETHER TO DIVERSIFY

1 I have defined high rates of protest use as 20 percent and above. This means that groups that use protest in more than one out of five of their events are considered to use high levels of protest. The same operationalization is used to determine high levels of electoral activity.

2 For more information about the coding of survival, see the Methodological Appendix.

3 Groups that used five or more different tactics over time were operationalized as diverse. The tactics were coded as follows: protest/march/rally, town hall, conference/speaker, organizational meeting, canvassing, press conference, fundraiser, strike, social event, petition, and other.

4 I coded each event as one of eleven tactics (as listed in note 3). Protests, marches, and rallies were combined into a single measure. Electoral tactics included any activity that was directed at elected leaders or elections. This included most of the town halls, canvassing, and petitions. However, it did not include all of the events in these categories. For example, if there was a petition to change police policy in a city or to rename a school named after a Confederate soldier, this was not coded as electoral. The protest events were coded as electoral if they were aimed at elected leaders and policies, such as the march against the Muslim ban. However, other events, such as the Women's

Marches themselves, were not coded as electoral as they were not primarily focused on electing or lobbying officials.

5 The Pasadena supercoalition activists also mentioned the organizing materials and strategies of the national Indivisible organization as inspiring their actions and organizational models. The other groups in this study did not explicitly mention responding to the national organization in their local organizing.

6 This finding supports Minkoff's research (1999) on organizations focused on women and racial minorities. She finds that groups that are in more crowded environments benefit from specialization and are more likely to survive over time.

CHAPTER 3. CREATING A VIBRANT CIVIL SOCIETY

1 I conducted the Qualitative Comparative Analysis (QCA) in order to understand the multiple pathways to survival in different contexts (Cress and Snow, 2000; Ragin, 1987). There are five main variables in the analysis in this chapter: support for existing activist groups (supportactgroups), engagement with civil society groups (civilsociety), history of activism (historyofactivism), group survival, and level of mobilization. Support for existing activist groups and engagement with civil society were both constructed based on the coding of the Facebook pages and the qualitative interviews with activists. Some groups explicitly discussed how they worked to support local activist groups, which were often groups that existed long before the first Women's March. Other groups did not mention an intentional strategy of partnering with existing groups in the community. In addition, groups differed in the extent to which they partnered with nonpolitical civil society allies, such as religious institutions, businesses, charities, and the local library. This was coded based on the Facebook listings of events, which listed the names of coalition partners, and the interviews with activists. Both of these variables were coded 1 (condition present) or 0 (condition not present).

The two outcomes of interest are group survival and the level of mobilization. I operationalize "survival" with two key elements. In order to be coded as still active in January 2018, a group had to have held an event within the last two months and to have at least two comments on its page within the past two months. To be coded as active in January 2019, the same criteria were used for the preceding two months. These groups were coded as "surviving" (1). All groups that were coded as "surviving" far surpassed this threshold, holding more events and having more comments in the time period. Group events was based on a count of all events hosted by the group in the two-year period. I then compared the number for each group to the overall average. If the group was above the average, it was coded 1. If it was below the average, it was coded 0. (For a similar coding strategy, see McCammon et al., 2001.)

2 Past research has consistently shown that areas with certain demographic features, such as higher levels of educational attainment and socioeconomic

status, tend to have higher levels of political engagement. Putnam (2019), for example, found that areas with higher educational attainment had more Indivisible groups founded on average. As a result, groups in these areas also tended to have more social movement organizations available for coalitions. The demographic variation across local contexts is an important part of why some areas are more conducive to coalitions than others.

3 Atlanta and Bridgeport also used similar supercoalition strategies. This chapter, however, focuses on the mobilization in Pittsburgh and Pasadena. That is because these cities offer model cases of how coalitions were used in contexts with long histories of activism and allows for a more in-depth consideration of these two cases. More information on Atlanta and Bridgeport is available in Corrigall-Brown (2019).

4 See table 3.2 for information on coalition use, event numbers, and survival by group and city.

CHAPTER 4. BECOMING INDIVISIBLE

1 Klandermans's second step in micro-mobilization involves recruitment networks and mobilization attempts. Mobilization attempts can occur through mass media, mail, and ties to organizations and other individuals (especially friends) (Klandermans and Oegema, 1987). Because this book focuses on groups who mobilize online, particularly through Facebook pages, there was little variation in the mobilization methods to examine. Larger strategies of how the groups worked to increase, diversify, or connect to other networks of activists through coalitions are discussed in more detail in chapter 3.

2 Meetings are central to organizational maintenance activity but are rarely studied in social movements. Most work on the role of meetings focuses on the workplace, where engagement in meetings has been associated with employee job satisfaction (Rogelberg et al., 2010). Research on meetings in social movement or other voluntary organizations has focused predominantly on the ways that leaders engage in meetings, the proportion of their time spent on this activity, and the ways that this shapes leader satisfaction (Baggetta et al., 2012; Baggetta et al., 2013; McCarthy and Wolfson, 1996).

3 Training was also a critical part of what occurred in some of the larger supercoalitions, discussed in more detail in chapter 3.

4 This chapter relies on a novel form of data that enabled me to trace the engagement of each Facebook page participant over time. Each Facebook user has a unique identifying number. For the first year under examination, I was able to record the identification number of each participant on the pages who posted or said they were interested in or going to an event. I did this using Facebook's own registered application for this process, enabling them to see what data I was collecting. I then learned how many times each person posted, said they were interested in a topic, or said they were going to an event. I used these data to

create a profile of attendance for each group. I always aggregated this information, and I never recorded additional information about a single person or viewed individuals' profiles. After the first year, Facebook changed its policy of data collection, as a result of a number of problematic issues with for-profit groups unethically collecting data. Because of this, I no longer collected these data after the first year.

5 The importance of open Facebook pages is discussed in more detail in chapter 5 on online engagement. The issue foci of groups is discussed in more detail in chapter 1.

REFERENCES

Acker, Lizzy. 2019. "DOJ Criminal Division Investigating Missing 2017 Portland Women's March Funds." *Oregon Live.* January 30. www.oregonlive.com.

Alinsky, Saul. 1971. *Rules for Radicals.* New York: Random House.

Andrews, Kenneth T., Neal Caren, and Alyssa Browne. 2018. "Protesting Trump." *Mobilization* 23(4): 393–400.

Armstrong, Elizabeth A., and Mary Bernstein. 2008. "Culture, Power, and Institutions: A Multi-institutional Politics Approach to Social Movements." *Sociological Theory* 26(1): 74–99.

Avigur-Eshel, Amit, and Izhak Berkovich. 2017. "Using Facebook Differently in Two Education Policy Protests." *Transforming Government: People, Process and Policy* 11(4): 596–611.

Baggetta, Matthew, Hahrie Han, and Kenneth T. Andrews. 2013. "Leading Associations: How Individual Characteristics and Team Dynamics Generate Committed Leaders." *American Sociological Review* 78(4): 544–573.

Baggetta, Matthew, Chaeyoon Lim, Kenneth T. Andrews, Marshall Ganz, and Hahrie C. Han. 2012. "Learning Civic Leadership: Leader Skill Development in the Sierra Club," pp. 110–113, in *Interest Group Politics*, 8th ed., ed. A. J. Cigler and B. A. Loomis. Los Angeles: CQ Press.

Barkan, S., S. Cohn, and W. Whitaker. 1995. "Beyond Recruitment: Predictors of Differential Participation in a National Antihunger Organization." *Sociological Forum* 10(1): 113–134.

Beamish, T. D., and A. J. Luebbers. 2009. "Alliance Building across Social Movements: Bridging Difference in a Peace and Justice Coalition." *Social Problems* 56(4): 647–676.

Beckett, Megan, Maxine Weinstein, Noreen Goldman, and Lin Yu-Husan. 2000. "Do Health Interview Surveys Yield Reliable Data on Chronic Illness among Older Respondents?" *American Journal of Epidemiology* 151: 315–323.

Beckwith, Karen. 2000. "Hinges in Collective Action: Strategic Innovation in the Pittston Coal Strike." *Mobilization* 5: 179–199.

Bennett, D., and P. Fielding. 1999. *The Net Effect: How Cyberadvocacy Is Changing the Political Landscape.* Merrifield, VA: e-advocates Press.

Bennett, W. L., and A. Segerberg. 2013. *The Logic of Connective Action: Digital Media and the Personalization of Contentious Politics.* Cambridge: Cambridge University Press.

Berger, P. L., and T. Luckmann. 1967. *The Social Construction of Reality: A Treatise in the Sociology of Knowledge*. New York, NY: Anchor.

Bernstein, Mary. 1997. "Celebration and Suppression: The Strategic Uses of Identity by the Lesbian and Gay Movement." *American Journal of Sociology* 103: 531–565.

Berry, Marie, and Erica Chenoweth. 2018. "Who Made the Women's March?," pp. 75–89, in *The Resistance*, ed. Davis S. Meyer and Sidney Tarrow. New York: Oxford University Press.

Beyerlein, Kraig, and John R. Hipp. 2006. "A Two-Stage Model for a Two-Stage Process: How Biographical Availability Matters for Social Movement Mobilization." *Mobilization* 11(3): 219–240.

Beyerlein, Kraig, Peter Ryan, Aliyah Abu-Hazeem, and Amity Pauley. 2018. "The 2017 Women's March: A National Study of Solidarity Events." *Mobilization* 23(4): 425-49.

Bimber, B., A. J. Flanagin, and C. Stohl. 2012. *Collective Action in Organizations: Interaction and Engagement in an Era of Technological Change*. Cambridge: Cambridge University Press.

Binder, Amy. 2002. *Contentious Curricula*. Princeton, NJ: Princeton University Press.

Blee, Kathleen. 2012. "Social Movement Audiences." *Sociological Forum* 27(1): 1–20.

Boudreau, M. C., and D. Robey. 2005. "Enacting Integrated Information Technology: A Human Agency Perspective." *Organization Science* 16(1): 3–18.

Brickell, Chris. 2000. "Heroes and Invaders: Gay and Lesbian Pride Parades and the Public/Private Distinction in New Zealand Media Accounts." *Gender, Race, and Culture* 7: 163–178.

Brockett, Charles D. 1991. "The Structure of Political Opportunities and Peasant Mobilization in Central America." *Comparative Politics* 23: 253–274.

Brooker, Megan E. 2018. "Indivisible," pp. 162–184, in *The Resistance: The Dawn of the Anti-Trump Opposition Movement*, ed. David S. Meyer and Sidney Tarrow. New York: Oxford University Press.

Buchanan, Larry, Quoctrung Bui, and Jugal K. Patel. 2020. "Black Lives Matter May Be the Largest Movement in U.S. History." *New York Times*. July 3.

Cardoso, Ana, Marie-Claude Boudreau, and João Álvaro Carvalho. 2019. "Organizing Collective Action: Does Information and Communication Technology Matter?" *Information and Organization* 29(3): 1–21.

Caren, Neal, Kay Jowers, and Sarah Gaby. 2012. "A Social Movement Online Community: Stormfront and the White Nationalist Movement," pp. 163–193, in *Media, Movements, and Political Change, Research in Social Movements, Conflicts and Change*, vol. 33, ed. Jennifer Earl and Deana A. Rohlinger. Bingley, UK: Emerald Publishing.

Carmin, Joann, and Deborah B. Balser. 2002. "Selecting Repertoires of Action in Environmental Movement Organizations." *Organizations and Environment* 15(4): 365–380.

Chenoweth, Erica. 2017. "This Is What We Learned by Counting the Women's Marches." *Washington Post*. February 7. www.washingtonpost.com.

Christens, Brian D., and Paul W. Speers. 2011. "Contextual Influences on Participation in Community Organizing: A Multilevel Longitudinal Study." *American Journal of Community Psychology* 47: 253–263.

Codur, Anne-Marie, and Mary Elizabeth King. 2015. "Women in Civil Resistance," pp. 401–406, in *Women, War and Non-violence: Topography, Resistance and Hope*, ed. Mariam M. Kurtz and Lester R. Kurtz. Santa Barbara, CA: Prager.

Cohn, S., S. Barkan, and W. Halteman. 2003. "Dimensions of Participation in a Social Movement Organization." *Sociological Inquiry* 73: 311–337.

Corrigall-Brown, Catherine. 2012. *Patterns of Protest: Trajectories of Participation in Social Movements*. Stanford, CA: Stanford University Press.

———. 2019. "'Regroup, Recharge, and Resist': How Modern Activists Mobilize in Difficult Contexts," pp. 47–68, in *The Future of Social Movements in Canada*, ed. Robert Brym. Oakville, Canada: Rock's Mills Press.

Cress, Daniel M., and David A. Snow. 2000. "The Outcomes of Homeless Mobilization." *American Journal of Sociology* 105: 1063–1104.

Crossley, Alison Dahl. 2014. "Facebook Feminism: Social Media, Blogs, and New Technologies of Contemporary U.S. Feminism." *Mobilization* 20(2): 253–268.

Davidson, Lee, and Thomas Burr. 2017. "Trump Greeted by Cheers and Protests as He Visits Utah, Trims 2 Million Acres from Bear Ears and Grand Staircase-Escalante National Monuments." *Salt Lake Tribune*. December 5. www.sltrib.com.

Della Porta, Donatella, and Lorenzo Mosca. 2005. "Global-net for Global Movements? A Network of Networks for a Movement of Movements." *Journal of Public Policy* 25(1): 165–190.

Earl, Jennifer, and Katrina Kimport. 2011. *Digitally Enabled Social Change: Activism in the Internet Age*. Cambridge, MA: MIT Press.

Earl, Jennifer, and Alan Schussman. 2003. "The New Site of Activism: On-line Organizations, Movement Entrepreneurs, and the Changing Location of Social Movement Decision Making." *Research in Social Movements, Conflicts and Change* 24: 155–187.

Eaton, Marc. 2010. "Manufacturing Community in an Online Activist Organization." *Information, Communication and Society* 13(2): 174–192.

Edwards, Bob, and Sam Marullo. 1995. "Organizational Mortality in a Declining Social Movement: The Demise of Peace Movement Organizations in the End of the Cold War Era." *American Sociological Review* 60(6): 908–927.

Einwohner, Rachel L., and Elle Rochford. 2019. "After the March: Using Instagram to Perform and Sustain the Women's March." *Sociological Forum* 34(S1): 1090–1111.

Eisinger, P. K. 1973. "The Conditions of Protest Behavior in American Cities." *American Political Science Review* 67: 11–28.

Fantasia, Rick. 1988. *Cultures of Solidarity: Consciousness, Action and Contemporary American Workers*. Berkeley: University of California Press.

Ferree, Myra Max, and Aili Mari Tripp, eds. 2006. *Global Feminism: Transnational Women's Activism, Organizing, and Human Rights*. New York: New York University Press.

Fisher, Dana. 2012. "Youth Political Participation: Bridging Activism and Electoral Politics." *Annual Review of Sociology* 38(2): 119–137.

———. 2019. *American Resistance: From the Women's March to the Blue Wave*. New York: Columbia University Press.

Fisher, Dana R., Dawn M. Dow, and Rashawn Ray. 2017. "Intersectionality Takes It to the Streets: Mobilizing across Diverse Interests for the Women's March." *Science Advances* 3: 9: eaao1390. https://doi.org/10.1126/sciadv.aao1390.

Fisher, Dana R., and Lorien Jasny. 2019. "Understanding Persistence in the Resistance." *Sociological Forum* 34(S1): 1065–1089.

Fisher, Dana R., Lorien Jasny, and Dawn M. Dow. 2018. "Why Are We Here? Patterns of Intersectional Motivations across the Resistance." *Mobilization* 23(4): 451–468.

Foster-Fishman, P. G., S. J. Pierce, and L. A. Van Egeren. 2009. "Who Participates and Why: Building a Process Model of Citizen Participation." *Health Education and Behavior: The Official Publication of the Society for Public Health Education* 36(3): 550–569. doi:10.1177/1090198108317408.

Fung, A., H. Russon Gilman, and J. Shkabatur. 2013. "Six Models for the Internet Politics." *International Studies Review* 15(1): 30–47.

Gamson, Joshua. 1996. "The Organizational Shaping of Collective Identity: The Case of Lesbian and Gay Film Festivals in New York." *Sociological Forum* 11: 231–261.

Gamson, William A. 1975. *The Strategy of Social Protest*. Homewood, IL: Dorsey Press.

Gamson, William A., and B. Fireman. 1979. "Utilitarian Logic in the Resource Mobilization Perspective," pp. 8–45, in *The Dynamics of Social Movements*, ed. M. N. Zald and J. M. McCarthy. Cambridge: Winthrop.

———. 2004. "Why David Sometimes Wins: Strategic Capacity in Social Movements," pp. 177–198, in: *Rethinking Social Movements: Structure, Meaning and Emotion*, ed. J. Goodwin and J. M. Jasper. New York: Rowman and Littlefield.

———. 2009. *Why David Sometimes Wins*. New York: Oxford University Press.

Gerbaudo, P. 2012. *Tweets and the Streets: Social Media and Contemporary Activism*. London: Pluto Press.

Giugni, Marco. 1988. "Was It Worth the Effort? The Outcomes and Consequences of Social Movements." *Annual Review of Sociology* 24: 371–393.

Goldstone, Jack A., ed. 2003. *States, Parties, and Social Movements*. Cambridge: Cambridge University Press.

Goodwin, Jeff, and James M. Jasper. 2004. "Emotions and Social Movements," pp. 611–635, in *The Handbook of the Sociology of Emotions*, ed. Jan E. Stets and Jonathan H. Turner. Boston: Springer.

Goodwin, Jeff, James Jasper, and Francesca Polletta. 2001. "Why Emotions Matter," pp. 1–24, in *Passionate Politics*, ed. Jeff Goodwin, James Jasper, and Francesca Polletta. Chicago: University of Chicago Press.

Gose, Leah E., and Theda Skocpol. 2019. "Resist, Persist, and Transform: The Emergence and Impact of Grassroots Resistance Groups Opposing the Trump Presidency." *Mobilization* 24(3): 293–317.

Greenberg, Leah, and Ezra Levin. 2019. *We Are Indivisible: A Blueprint for Democracy after Trump*. New York: Simon and Schuster.

Han, Hahrie. 2014. *How Organizations Develop Activists: Civic Associations and Leadership in the 21st Century*. Oxford: Oxford University Press.

Harlow, S., and D. Harp. 2012. "Collective Action on the Web: A Cross-Cultural Study of Social Networking Sites and Online and Offline Activism in the US and Latin America." *Information, Communication and Society* 15(2): 196–216.

Hathaway, Will, and David S. Meyer. 1993. "Competition and Cooperation in Social Movement Coalitions: Lobbying for Peace in the 1980s." *Berkeley Journal of Sociology* 38: 157–183.

Hersh, Eitan. 2020. *Politics Is for Power: How to Move beyond Political Hobbyism, Take Action, and Make Real Change*. New York: Simon and Schuster.

Houston, J. D., and N. R. Todd. 2013. "Religious Congregations and Social Justice Participation: A Multilevel Examination of Social Processes and Leadership." *American Journal of Community Psychology* 52(3–4): 273–287. doi:10.1007/s10464-013-9593-3.

Indivisible.org. 2020. "Who We Are." https://indivisible.org/#.

Jasper, James. 2011. "Emotions and Social Movements: Twenty Years of Theory and Research." *Annual Review of Sociology* 37: 285–303.

Jenkins, J. Craig. 1982. "The Transformation of a Constituency into a Movement," pp. 52–70, in *The Social Movements of the 1960s and 1970s*, ed. J. Freeman. New York: Longmans.

Jenkins, J. Craig, David Jacobs, and Jon Agnone. 2003. "Political Opportunities and African-American Protest, 1948–1997." *American Journal of Sociology* 109: 277–303.

Jenkins, J. Craig, and Chuck Perrow. 1977. "Insurgency of the Powerless: Farm Workers Movements (1946–1972)." *American Sociological Review* 42: 249–268.

Kitschelt, Herbert. 1986. "Political Opportunity Structures and Political Protest: Antinuclear Movements in Four Democracies." *British Journal of Political Science* 16: 57–85.

Klandermans, Bert. 1984. "Mobilization and Participation: Social-Psychological Expansions of Resource Mobilization Theory." *American Sociological Review* 49(5): 583–600.

———. 1988. "The Formation and Mobilization of Consensus." *International Social Movement Research* 1: 173–196.

———. 1993. "A Theoretical Framework for Comparisons of Social Movement Participation." *Sociological Forum* 8(3): 383–402.

Klandermans, Bert, and Dirk Oegema. 1987. "Potentials, Networks, Motivations, and Barriers: Steps towards Participation in Social Movements." *American Sociological Review* 52(4): 519–531.

Klandermans, B., J. van Stekelenburg, M. L. Damen, D. van Troost, and A. van Leeuwen. 2014. "Mobilization without Organization: The Case of Unaffiliated Demonstrators." *European Sociological Review* 30(6): 702–716. https://doi.org/10.1093/esr/jcu068.

Knoke, D. 1988. "Incentives in Collective Action Organizations." *American Sociological Review* 53: 311–329.

Kriesi, H., W. Saris, and A. Wille. 1993. "Mobilization Potential for Environmental Protest." *European Sociological Review* 9(2): 155–172.

Kucinskas, Jaime. 2014. "The Unobtrusive Tactics of Religious Movements." *Sociology of Religion* 75(4): 537–550.

Leighley, Jan. 1996. "Group Membership and the Mobilization of Political Participation." *Journal of Politics* 58(2): 447–463.

Levi, M., and G. H. Murphy. 2006. "Coalitions of Contention: The Case of the WTO Protests in Seattle." *Political Studies* 54(4): 651–670.

Lichterman, Paul. 2005. *Elusive Togetherness: Church Groups Trying to Bridge America's Divisions*. Princeton, NJ: Princeton University Press.

Lobera, Josep, and Martin Portos. 2020. "Decentralizing Electoral Campaigns? New-Old Parties, Grassroots and Digital Activism." *Information, Communication and Society* 24(10): 1–22.

Markus, Gregory B. 1986. "Stability and Change in Political Attitudes: Observed, Recalled, and 'Explained.' " *Political Behavior* 8: 21–44.

Maton, K. I. 2008. "Empowering Community Settings: Agents of Individual Development, Community Betterment, and Positive Social Change." *American Journal of Community Psychology* 41: 4–21.

McAdam, Doug. 1982. *Political Process and the Development of Black Insurgency, 1930–1970*. Chicago: University of Chicago Press.

———. 1983. "Tactical Innovation and the Pace of Insurgency." *American Sociological Review* 48: 735–754.

———. 1986. "Recruitment to High-Risk Activism: The Case of Freedom Summer." *American Journal of Sociology* 92(1): 64–90.

———. 1996. "Movement Strategy and Dramaturgic Framing in Democratic States: The Case of the American Civil Rights Movement." *Research on Democracy and Society* 3: 155–176.

McAdam, Doug, and D. Rucht. 1993. "The Cross-National Diffusion of Movement Ideas." *Annals of the American Academy of Political and Social Science* 528: 56–87.

McAdam, Doug, and Sidney Tarrow. 2010. "Ballots and Barricades: On the Reciprocal Relationships between Elections and Social Movements." *Perspectives on Politics* 8(2): 529–542.

McAdam, Doug, Sidney Tarrow, and Charles Tilly. 2001. *Dynamics of Contention*. Cambridge: Cambridge University Press.

McCammon, Holly J. 2003. "Out of the Parlors and into the Streets: The Changing Tactic Repertoire of the U.S. Women's Suffrage Movements." *Social Forces* 81(3): 787–818.

McCammon, Holly J., and Karen E. Campbell. 2002. "Allies on the Road to Victory: Coalition Formation between the Suffragists and the Woman's Christian Temperance Union." *Mobilization* 7(3): 231–251.

McCammon, Holly J., Karen E. Campbell, Ellen M. Granberg, and Christine Mowery. 2001. "How Movements Win: Gendered Opportunity Structures and U.S. Women's Suffrage Movements, 1866 to 1919." *American Sociological Review* 66: 49–70.

McCarthy, John D., David W. Britt, and Mark Wolfson. 1991. "The Institutional Channeling of Social Movements in the Modern State." *Research in Social Movements,
Conflicts, and Change* 13: 45–76.

McCarthy, John D., and Edward T. Walker. 2004. "Alternative Organizational Repertoires of Poor People's Social Movement Organizations." *Non-profit and Volunteer
Sector Quarterly* 33: 97S–119S.

McCarthy, John D., and Mark Wolfson. 1992. "Consensus Movements, Conflict Movement, and the Cooptation of Civic and State Infrastructures," pp. 273–297, in *Fron-
tiers in Social Movement Theory*, ed. Aldon D. Morris and Carol McClurg Mueller.
Binghamton, NY: Vail-Ballou Press.

———. 1996. "Resource Mobilization by Local Social Movement Organizations:
Agency, Strategy, and Organization in the Movement against Drinking and Driving." *American Sociological Review* 61: 1070–1088.

McKane, Rachel G., and Holly J. McCammon. 2018. "Why We March: The Role of
Grievances, Threats, and Movement Organizational Resources in the 2017 Women's
Marches." *Mobilization* 23(4): 401–424. https://doi.org/10.17813/1086-671X-23-4-401.

Meikle, G. 2016. *Social Media: Communication, Sharing and Visibility*. New York:
Routledge.

Melucci, Alberto. 1989. *Nomads of the Present: Social Movements and Individual Needs
in Contemporary Society*. Los Angeles: Hutchinson Radius.

Mercea, D. 2013. "Probing the Implications of Facebook Use for the Organizational
Form of Social Movement Organizations." *Information, Communication and Society*
16(8): 1306–1327.

Meyer, David S. 1999. "Tending the Vineyard: Cultivating Political Process Research."
Sociological Forum 14: 79–92.

———. 2004. "Protest and Political Opportunity." *Annual Review of Sociology* 30: 125–145.

———. 2006. "Claiming Credit: Stories of Movement Influence as Outcomes." *Mobilization* 11(3): 281–298.

Meyer, David S., and Steven Boutcher. 2007. "Signals and Spillover: *Brown v. Board of
Education* and Other Social Movements." *Perspectives on Politics* 50(1): 81–93.

Meyer, David S., and Catherine Corrigall-Brown. 2005. "Coalitions and Political
Context: U.S. Movements against Wars in Iraq." *Mobilization* 10(3): 327–344.

Meyer, David S., and Suzanne Staggenborg. 2008. "Opposing Movement Strategies in
U.S. Abortion Politics," pp. 207–238, in *Research in Social Movements, Conflict and
Change*, ed. P. G. Coy. Bingley, UK: Emerald Publishing.

Meyer, David S., and Sidney Tarrow. 2018. *The Resistance: The Dawn of the Anti-Trump
Opposition Movement*. New York: Oxford University Press.

Meyer, David S., and Nancy Whittier. 1994. "Social Movement Spillover." *Social Problems* 41(2): 277–298.

Minkoff, Debra C. 1999. "Bending with the Wind: Strategic Change and Adaptation by
Women's and Racial Minority Organizations." *American Journal of Sociology* 101:
1592–1627.

Molyneau, Maxine. 1998. "Analysing Women's Movements." *Development and Change* 29(2): 219–245.

Morris, Aldon. 1984. *The Origins of the Civil Rights Movement: Black Communities Organizing for Change*. New York: Free Press.

———. 1993. "Birmingham Confrontation Reconsidered: An Analysis of the Dynamics and Tactics of Mobilization." *American Journal of Sociology* 58(5): 621–636.

Murphy, Gillian. 2005. "Coalitions and the Development of the Global Environmental Movement: A Double-Edged Sword." *Mobilization* 10(2): 235–250.

Myers, Daniel J. 1994. "Communication Technology and Social Movements: Contributions of Computer Networks to Activism." *Social Science Computer Review* 12(2): 251–260.

Nepstad, Sheron Erickson. 2004. "Persistent Resistance: Commitment and Community in the Plowshares Movement." *Social Problems* 51: 43–60.

Oberschall, Anthony. 1973. *Social Conflict and Social Movements*. Englewood Cliffs, NJ: Prentice-Hall.

Oegema, Dirk, and Bert Klandermans. 1994. "Why Social Movement Sympathizers Don't Participate: Erosion and Non-conversion of Support." *American Sociological Review* 59(5): 703–722.

Olson, Mancur. 1965. *The Logic of Collective Action: Public Goods and the Theory of Groups*. Cambridge, MA: Harvard University Press.

Olzak, Susan, and Erik W. Johnson 2019. "The Risk of Occupying a Broad Niche for Environmental Social Movement Organizations." *Mobilization* 24(2): 177–198.

Opp, Karl Dieter. 1983. *Soft Incentives and Collective Action: Some Results of a Survey on the Conditions of Participating in the Anti-nuclear Movement*. Hamburg: Institut fur Soziologie.

Pamplin Media Group. 2017. "Portland Women's March Brings Together Thousands Who Want 'a Better World.'" *Portland Tribune*. January 21.

Passy, Florence, and Marco Giugni. 2001. "Social Networks and Individual Perceptions: Explaining Differential Participation in Social Movements." *Sociological Forum* 16(1): 123–153.

Pellow, David N. 1999. "Framing Emerging Environmental Movement Tactics: Mobilizing Consensus, Demobilizing Conflict." *Sociological Forum* 14(4): 649–683.

Piven, Frances Fox, and R. A. Cloward. 1977. *Poor People's Movements: How They Succeed and How They Fail*. New York: Vintage.

Polletta, Francesca. 2002. *Freedom Is an Endless Meeting*. Chicago: University of Chicago Press.

Pousadela, Ines M. 2016. "Social Mobilization and Political Representation: The Women's Movement's Struggle for Legal Abortion in Uruguay." *Voluntas* 27: 125–145.

Principe, Marie A. 2016. *Women in Nonviolent Movements*. Special Report 399. Washington, DC: United States Institute of Peace.

Pullum, Amanda. 2017. "Foul Weather Friends: Enabling Movement Alliance through an Intentionally Limited Coalition." *Social Currents* 5(3): 228–243.

Putnam, Lara. 2019. "In Pennsylvania's Exurbs and Urban Suburbs, Political Organizing Has Been Intense Since 2016. What Could It Mean for 2020?" American Communities Project. August 6. www.americancommunities.org.

Ragin, Charles C. 1987. *The Comparative Method: Moving beyond Qualitative and Quantitative Strategies*. Berkeley: University of California Press.

Reger, Jo, and Suzanne Staggenborg. 2006. "Patterns of Mobilization in Local Movement Organizations: Leadership and Strategy in Four National Organization for Women Chapters." *Sociological Perspectives* 49(3): 297–323.

Robnett, Belinda. 1981. "African-American Women in the Civil Rights Movement, 1954–1965: Gender, Leadership, and Micromobilization." *American Journal of Sociology* 101(6): 1661–1693.

Rogelberg, Steven G., Joseph A. Allen, Linda Shanock, Cliff Scott, and Marissa Shuffler. 2010. "Employee Satisfaction with Meetings: A Contemporary Facet of Job Satisfaction." *Human Resource Management* 49: 149–172.

Roig-Tierno, Norat, Tomas F. Gonzalez-Cruz, and Jordi Llopis-Martinez. 2017. "An Overview of Qualitative Comparative Analysis." *Journal of Innovation and Knowledge* 2(1): 15–23.

Rose, F. 2000. *Coalitions across the Class Divide: Lessons from the Labor, Peace, and Environmental Movements*. Ithaca, NY: Cornell University Press.

Schacter, Daniel L. 1996. *Searching for Memory: The Brain, the Mind, and the Past*. New York: Basic Books.

Schmitt, Frederika E., and Patricia Yancey Martin. 1999. "Unobtrusive Mobilization by an Institutionalized Rape Crisis Center." *Gender and Society* 13(3): 364–384.

Schussman, A., and S. Soule. 2005. "Process and Protest: Accounting for Individual Protest Participation." *Social Forces* 84(2): 1083–1108.

Scott, Jacqueline, and Duane Alwin. 1998. "Retrospective versus Prospective Measurement of Life Histories in Longitudinal Research," pp. 98–127, in *Methods of Research: Qualitative and Quantitative Approaches*, ed. G. Elder Jr. and J. Ziele. Thousand Oaks, CA: Sage.

Senier, Laura, Brian Mayer, Phil Brown, and Rachel Morello-Frosch. 2007. "School Custodians and Green Cleaners: New Approaches to Labor-Environment Coalitions." *Organizations and Environment* 20(3): 304–324.

Shapiro, Thomas M. 1985. "Structure and Process in Social Movement Strategy: The Movement against Sterilization Abuse." *Research in Social Movements, Conflicts, and Change* 8: 87–108.

Shirky, C. 2008. *Here Comes Everybody: The Power of Organizing without Organizations*. New York: Penguin.

Shultziner, D. 2010. *Struggling for Recognition: The Psychological Impetus for Democratic Progress*. New York: Continuum Press.

Shultziner, D., and S. Goldberg. 2019. "The Stages of Mass Mobilization: Separate Phenomenon and Distinct Causal Mechanisms." *Journal of Theory and Social Behavior* 49: 2–23.

Singh, Jitendra, and Charles Lumsden. 1990. "Theory and Research in Organizational Ecology." *Annual Review of Sociology* 16: 161–195.

Skocpol, Theda, and Caroline Tervo, eds. 2019. *Upending American Politics: Polarizing Parties, Ideological Elites, and Citizen Activists from the Tea Party to the Anti-Trump Resistance.* New York: Oxford University Press.

Snow, David A., E. Rochford Jr., S. Worden, and R. Benford. 1986. "Frame Alignment Processes, Micromobilization, and Movement Participation." *American Sociological Review* 51(4): 464–481.

Snow, David A., Louis A. Zurcher, and Sheldon Ekland-Olson. 1980. "Social Networks and Social Movements: A Microstructural Approach to Differential Recruitment." *American Sociological Review* 45: 787–780.

Soule, Sarah A., and Susan Olzak. 2004. "When Do Movements Matter? The Politics of Contingency and the Equal Rights Amendment." *American Sociological Review* 69: 473–497.

Staggenborg, Suzanne. 1986. "Coalition Work in the Pro-choice Movement: Organizational and Environmental Opportunities and Obstacles." *Social Problems* 33(5): 375–390.

———. 1988. "The Consequences of Professionalization and Formalization in the Pro-choice Movement." *American Sociological Review* 53: 585–606.

———. 1989. "Stability and Innovation in the Women's Movement: A Comparison of Two Movement Organizations." *Social Problems* 36: 75–92.

———. 2015. "Event Coalitions in the Pittsburgh G20 Protests." *Sociological Quarterly* 56(2): 386–411.

Swidler, Ann. 1986. "Culture in Action: Symbols and Strategies." *American Sociological Review* 51: 273–286.

Tarrow, Sidney. 2004. "The New Transnational Activism." Unpublished manuscript. Ithaca, NY: Cornell University.

———. 2011. *Power in Movement.* Cambridge: Cambridge University Press.

Taylor, Verta. 1989. "Social Movement Continuity: The Women's Movement in Abeyance." *American Sociological Review* 54(5): 761–775.

Taylor, Verta, Nella Van Dyke, Katrina Kimport, and Ellen Ann Andersen. 2009. "Culture and Mobilization: Tactical Repertoires, Same-Sex Weddings, and the Impact on Gay Activism." *American Sociological Review* 74(6): 865–890.

Tesdahl, Eric A., and Paul W. Speer. 2015. "Organizational Level Predictors of Sustained Movement Participation." *American Journal of Community Psychology* 55: 48–57.

Tilly, Charles. 1978. *From Mobilization to Revolution.* Reading, MA: Addison-Wesley.

———. 2006. *Regimes and Repertoires.* Chicago: University of Chicago Press.

Toyama, K. 2010. "Can Technology End Poverty?" *Boston Review* 35(6).

Tufekci, Zeynep. 2017. *Twitter and Tear Gas: The Power and Fragility of Networked Protest.* New Haven, CT: Yale University Press.

Tufekci, Zeynep, and D. Freelon. 2013. "Introduction to the Special Issue on New Media and Social Unrest." *American Behavioral Scientist* 57(7): 843–847.

Tufekci, Zepnep, and C. Wilson. 2012. "Social Media and the Decision to Participation in Political Protest: Observations from Tahir Square." *Journal of Communication* 62: 363–379.

Valenzuela, S. 2013. "Unpacking the Use of Social Media for Protest Behavior." *American Behavioral Scientist* 57(7): 920–942.

Vanderford, M. L. 1989. "Vilification and Social Movements: A Case Study of Pro-life and Pro-choice Rhetoric." *Quarterly Journal of Speech* 75(2): 166–182.

Van Dyke, Nella. 2003. "Crossing Movement Boundaries: Factors That Facilitate Coalition Protest by American College Students, 1930–1990." *Social Problems* 50(2): 226–250.

Van Dyke, Nella, and B. Amos. 2017. "Social Movement Coalitions: Formation, Longevity, and Success." *Sociological Compass* 11(7): e12489.

Van Dyke, Nella, and Marc Dixon. 2013. "Activist Human Capital: Skills Acquisition and the Development of Commitment to Social Movement Activism." *Mobilization* 18(2): 197–212.

Van Dyke, Nella, and Holly J. McCammon, eds. 2010. *Strategic Alliances: Coalition Building and Social Movements.* Minneapolis: University of Minnesota Press.

Van Dyke, Nella, Sarah Soule, and Verta Taylor. 2004. "The Targets of Social Movements: Beyond a Focus on the State," pp. 27–51, in *Authority in Contention*, ed. Daniel Myers and Daniel Cress. Bingley, UK: Emerald Publishing.

Van Laer, J. 2010. "Activists Online and Offline: The Internet as an Information Channel for Protest Demonstrations." *Mobilization* 15(3): 347–366.

Vasi, I. B., and C. S. Suh. 2016. "Online Activities, Spatial Proximity, and the Diffusion of the Occupy Wall Street Movement in the United States." *Mobilization* 21(2): 139–154.

Viterna, Jocelyn. 2013. *Women in War.* Oxford: Oxford University Press.

Voss, Kim, and Rachel Sherman. 2000. "Breaking the Iron Law of Oligarchy: Union Revitalization in the American Labor Movement." *American Journal of Sociology* 106(2): 303–349.

Wang, Dan, Alessandro Piazza, and Sarah A. Soule. 2018. "Boundary-Spanning in Social Movements: Antecedents and Outcomes." *Annual Review of Sociology* 44: 167–187.

Ward, Matthew. 2016. "Rethinking Social Movement Micromobilization: Multi-stage Theory and the Role of Social Ties." *Current Sociology Review* 64(6): 853–874.

Warren, A. M., A. Sulaiman, and N. I. Jaafar. 2014. "Social Media Effects on Fostering Online Civic Engagement and Building Citizen Trust and Trust in Institutions." *Government Information Quarterly* 31(2): 291–301.

Whittier, Nancy. 2004. "The Consequences of Social Movements for Each Other," pp. 531–551, in *The Blackwell Companion to Social Movements*, ed. David A. Snow, Sarah A. Soule, and Hanspeter Kriesi. Malden, MA: Blackwell.

Women's March. 2017. "Sister Marches." www.womensmarchnetworks.org.

INDEX

ABOUT THE AUTHOR

CATHERINE CORRIGALL-BROWN is Professor and Head of Sociology at the University of British Columbia, Canada. She is the author of *Patterns of Protest: Trajectories of Participation in Social Movements* and *Imagining Sociology: An Introduction with Readings, Second Edition.* Her research focuses on participation in social movements, coalitions, funding, and framing. This research has appeared in *Social Forces, Sociological Perspectives,* the *International Journal of Comparative Sociology, Social Movement Studies,* and *Mobilization.*